T0268114

IMAGES
*of America*

# US 14TH CAVALRY
## AT HIGHWOOD AND
## FORT SHERIDAN

IMAGES
*of America*

# US 14TH CAVALRY
# AT HIGHWOOD AND
# FORT SHERIDAN

Bonnie Duresa

ARCADIA
PUBLISHING

Copyright © 2023 by Bonnie Duresa
ISBN 978-1-4671-0832-4

Published by Arcadia Publishing
Charleston, South Carolina

Printed in the United States of America

Library of Congress Control Number: 2023938123

For all general information, please contact Arcadia Publishing:
Telephone 843-853-2070
Fax 843-853-0044
E-mail sales@arcadiapublishing.com
For customer service and orders:
Toll-Free 1-888-313-2665

Visit us on the Internet at www.arcadiapublishing.com

*This book is in memory of my father-in-law, John Daniel Duresa (1912–1998), who served in the 14th Cavalry Regiment, Company B, at Fort Sheridan, and my beloved husband, Dr. Robert John Duresa (1934–2020), who served in the US Air Force. Throughout most of his professional career, he cared for developmentally disabled children. May he continue to rest in peace at Fort Sheridan National Cemetery.*

# CONTENTS

# ACKNOWLEDGMENTS

An author's name is printed predominately in a book, while other contributors go unknown. With that in mind, I wish to thank several wonderful people to whom I am indebted for aiding in compiling this book. One person who encouraged and motivated me to write this book was Michael J. Harkins. He is the president of the Barrington History Museum and a professor and department chairman of history at William Rainey Harper College. Michael assisted me greatly in organizing the military sections of the book.

Initially, I contacted Antoinette "Teta" Minuzzo, past president of the Highwood Historical Society (HHS) and archivist to assist with Highwood's history and association with Fort Sheridan. Her love of the city of Highwood extends back to 1960 while teaching at the Oak Terrace Elementary School. She has been involved with the HHS since 1996. Teta was unable to complete chapters one and two of this book as originally planned due to unforeseen circumstances.

Another thank you goes to Highwood Historical Society's members Tom Scopelliti and Shirley Fitzgerald, who both jumped in to help and complete gathering photographs and composing narratives needed to finalize the book. Tom and Shirley's dedication and talented abilities account for completing chapters one and two of this book, along with the help of Jack Johnson.

The Highwood Historical Society is the author of chapters one and two, including the descriptions. The photographs and images used were taken from the archives of the society. The author assumes no credit for these chapters.

All images in chapters three to six are courtesy of the author's family photographic collection. Most of the caption information was gathered from oral history notes by John D. Duresa in addition to research. Great care has been taken to make certain that the information in this book is correct. The author is fully aware that factual, typographical, and other errors can skip through even the most stringent vetting process. It is intended that this book be enjoyed for its photographic value of a bygone era when patriotism was very intense. May God bless the United States of America!

# INTRODUCTION

*The Nation Which Forgets Its Defenders Will Itself Be Forgotten.*

—Calvin Coolidge, 30th president of the United States

The memories of Fort Sheridan linger in the thousands of veterans, men, and women who trained and were stationed here. This book is about the 14th Cavalry Regiment of the 1930s at Fort Sheridan and its important connection with the village of Highwood, its people, and its businesses. Within the history of this association, very little credit was chronicled about this "quiet time." It is important to document these soldiers for their service at Fort Sheridan between the World Wars so all are recognized and not forgotten.

Step back in time with Pvt. John Daniel Duresa through his 1930s extensive collection of photographs and documents of this amazing journey with the 14th Cavalry Regiment of Fort Sheridan. Duresa, the author's future father-in-law, purchased these photographs from his meager salary of $25 a month. These photographs served as a remembrance of his experiences in the Army. The reader will also gain knowledge of the history of Highwood and how it played a significant role in the formation and support of Fort Sheridan and its soldiers. Duresa's photographs reveal the 14th Cavalry's training tactics, including military parades throughout the 1930s era of Chicago, passing its landmark buildings and streets and experiencing the thrills of Soldier Field war games and tournaments. Travel with the troops on their field hikes and exhibitions of military maneuvers at Fort Sheridan and through Illinois and Wisconsin. These young men were serving with patriotic spirit, enthusiasm, and discipline, which was depicted in these photographs during the quiet time between the World Wars of our military history. The Fort Sheridan troops were ready to train these eager recruits in the defense of our nation.

This unique historic trip in time begins with the founding of Fort Sheridan or Camp Highwood as originally identified in the 1887 deed: "Known as the Highwood tract, in Lake County, Illinois, containing five hundred ninety-eight and one-half acres, lying at Lake Michigan, north of the city of Chicago, and distance of twenty-five miles; this tract being a tract donated by the Commercial Club of Chicago." The Commercial Club was an organization of prominent businessmen with the express purpose of conveying the land to create an Army post for the Chicago area.

On November 8, 1887, Companies F and K of the US 6th Infantry troops from Fort Douglas, Utah, arrived with their commanding officer, Maj. William John Lyster. They exited from the Chicago & North Western Railway at the Highwood station and peered out over nearly 600 acres of uncleared land that stretched to the bluffs and beyond to Lake Michigan. For the first year, the soldiers cleared the land, survived heat and cold, and lived in tents with inadequate clothing, food, and equipment. Lyster attempted to acquire funding for the construction of the fort. It was not until 1889 that Congress appropriated $300,000 for the construction of permanent structures to accommodate six infantry companies and four cavalry troops on the base. Included in the allotted government money was the construction of a water tower, a wharf, a cemetery, and a rifle range. By the time Lyster gave up his command on September 2, 1890, construction of the fort was well underway.

The layout of Fort Sheridan was based on the traditional hollow square plan around a central parade ground. Contracts for the Army post-construction were the responsibility of Brig. Gen. Sam B. Holabird, quartermaster general of the Army. The general awarded his son's newly formed architectural firm of Holabird and Roche the contract to design Fort Sheridan. In 1896, a special act of Congress prohibited the employment of private firms to design military installations. No doubt Holabird hiring his son's architectural firm had prompted Congress to enact the law.

The US 14th Cavalry Regiment was not the first Army mounted force to arrive at the fort in 1920; it was one of the last. These cavalrymen were weary travelers who rode their faithful horses over 1,090 miles from Fort Sam Houston, Texas, north to the fort at Highwood. Upon the 14th Cavalry's arrival at Fort Sheridan, the men came with a wealth of combat knowledge under their belts. The fort was an ideal place for training for both recruits and Army reservists. Before this element of the US 14th Cavalry traveled to the fort, the regiment was admitted into the Army in 1901. Within months of the 14th Cavalry's organization, elements of the regiment occupied Fort Wingate, New Mexico Territory; Fort Gran, Arizona Territory; and Fort Logan, Colorado. In 1902, Troops E and H at Fort Logan accompanied Pres. Theodore Roosevelt in a parade in Denver. The 14th continued with deployment to the Philippines and returned there in 1909. After returning to the United States, the 14th Cavalry provided security for surveyors of our national parks and rendered assistance during the California earthquake and fire of 1906.

The 14th Cavalry Regiment, in 1916, along with other regiments under the command of Gen. John Joseph "Black Jack" Pershing, headed for Mexico. The large group was in search of Francisco "Pancho" Villa. The cavalry successively located the hostile Villa and his rebels. It was one of the largest US Cavalry horse-mounted campaigns ever. In 1918, the 14th intended to join combat operations at Camp Travis, Texas, and World War I, but the war had ended before their arrival. The troops returned to the Rio Grande and resumed duties of safeguarding our border.

The period of this book is during the 1930s Great Depression era. Aside from the Civil War and World War I, the Great Depression was the gravest crisis in American history. The widespread prosperity of the 1920s ended suddenly with the stock market crash in October 1929, and a great economic depression followed. The Depression threatened people's jobs, savings, and even their homes and farms. At the depths of the Depression, over one-quarter of the American workforce was out of work. For many Americans, these were hard times. During this difficult time, ambitious young men had trouble finding a job. Enlisting in the US Army was appealing to a special kind of young man. It provided them with adventure, steady income, shelter, and three square meals a day. It would also relieve their families of one less mouth to feed during these difficult times.

May God bless America and all the troops of gallant and patriotic men and women who served at Fort Sheridan and protected our Great Nation and Its Republic!

—Bonnie Duresa

## One

# HIGHWOOD,
# THE BEGINNINGS

The influx of early settlers to the areas that would become Highwood and Fort Sheridan began for the most part in the 1840s. Many of these were farmers, loggers, or land speculators. In 1847, John Hettinger and John Peterman platted the northeastern portion of Section 14, Range 12, 3rd Meridian in Deerfield Township, Lake County, Illinois. This area bordering Lake Michigan was named the village of St. John.

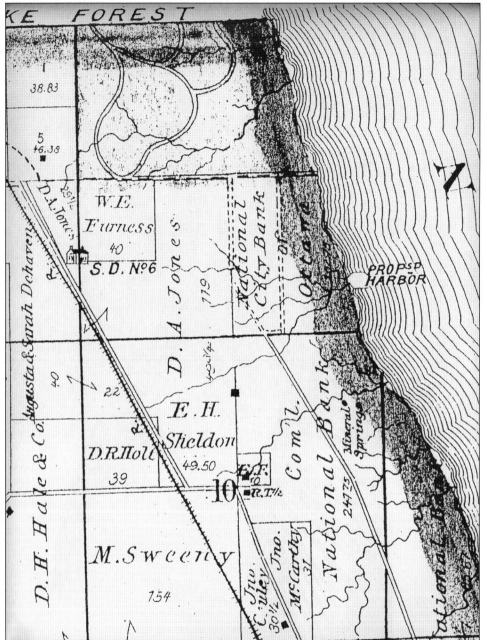

After years of legal disputes regarding the area, ownership of the property of St. John was transferred to Nathan and William Shepard. William Shepard eventually sold the land, as well as the land he owned, which extended to the north as far as the southern border of Lake Forest. The buyer was Samuel J. Walker, a prominent Chicago developer. Unfortunately, Walker was affected adversely by the Depression of 1873. At that time, he was the largest property owner in the Chicago area. Walker defaulted on loans, and his creditors, mainly the Commercial National Bank and the National Bank of Ottawa, seized the property. The lands are depicted on the map. The ownership of the land was contested in court, and it remained largely undeveloped until its designation as a military base called Camp Highwood and, later, Fort Sheridan.

In 1869, the Highland Park Building Company, consisting of prominent individuals from Chicago, platted and incorporated the city of Highland Park. One of these individuals was the highly respected minister of the First Baptist Church of Chicago, the Reverend William W. Everts. While serving in Louisville, he was so influential that he was credited by some as being the reason Kentucky remained in the Union during the Civil War. Highland Park bordered the newly platted village called Highwood, a village founded by Everts himself. Everts, along with Rev. Reuben Jeffery, filed the first plat map of Highwood on August 22, 1868. The map covered mostly the southeastern portion of the present community and contained approximately 55 acres of land. A portion of this map is shown. (Right, courtesy of the University of Illinois).

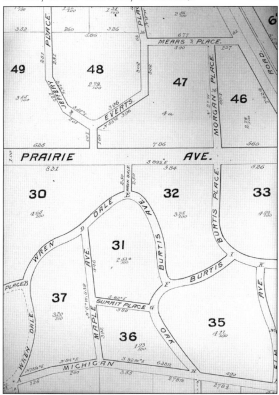

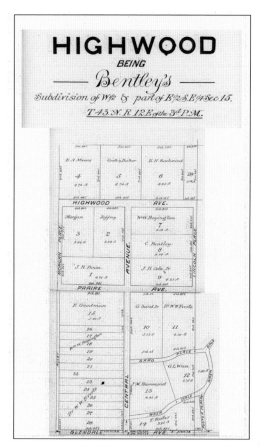

In 1868, Cyrus Bentley, a noted Chicago attorney, filed a plat map of the land in the southwestern section of Highwood. Under the supervision of Everts, Bentley acted as trustee for the new landowners, among which were Everts, his sons-in-law E. Ashley Mears and George L. Wrenn, and the celebrated architect William W. Boyington.

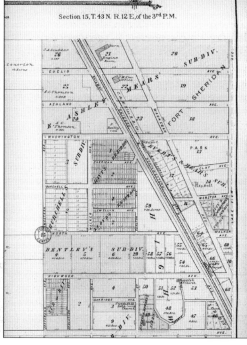

E. Ashley Mears later purchased land to the north originally owned by Joseph E. Burchell and Dennis Sophronia. The map, although from a later time, shows nearly the entire final product of the previous land purchases, a rectangular plat one-half square mile in area. This area was incorporated as the village of Highwood in 1887.

No. 36397. Filed for Record the 7th day of October A.D. 1887, at 11.50 o'clock A.M.

**This Indenture Witnesseth,** That the Grantors Edward Fitzgerald and Bridget Fitzgerald his wife

of the Town of Deerfield in the County of Lake and State of Illinois for the consideration of Two Thousand Dollars,

CONVEY AND QUIT-CLAIM to Adolphus C. Bartlett Charles L. Hutchinson John Janes

of the City of Chicago County of Cook and State of Illinois

all interest in the following described Real Estate, to-wit:

The North West ¼ of the South West ¼ of the North East ¼ of Section Ten (10) Town #3 North Range 12 East of the 3d PM

Situated in the County of Lake in the State of Illinois, hereby releasing and waiving all rights under and by virtue of the Homestead Exemption Laws of this State.

Dated this Ninth day of July A.D. 1887

Edward Fitzgerald [L.S.]
Bridget Fitzgerald [L.S.]
[L.S.]
[L.S.]

**STATE OF ILLINOIS,**
COUNTY OF Lake

Notarial Deed

George Fraser a Notary Public in and for the said County, in the State aforesaid, DO HEREBY CERTIFY, that Edward Fitzgerald and his wife Bridget Fitzgerald personally known to me to be the same persons whose name are subscribed to the foregoing instrument, appeared before me this day in person, and acknowledged that they signed, sealed and delivered the said instrument as their free and voluntary act, for the uses and purposes therein set forth, including the release and waiver of the right of homestead.

GIVEN under my hand and Notarial seal, this twelfth day of July A.D. 1887

George Fraser
Notary Public

During the financial panic of 1873, Samuel J. Walker defaulted on loans obtained from the Commercial National Bank and the National Bank of Ottawa. The properties in Chicago for which these loans were obtained were so encumbered that the banks decided to seek retribution by seizing other parcels of land from Walker. These properties, comprising 600 acres, were the lands originally owned by William Shepard, as described earlier. With fears of continued labor unrest, the Commercial Club of Chicago petitioned the secretary of war to obtain a tract of land near Chicago for a military base. In 1886, the board of Army officers determined that the land owned by the above banks was best suited for such a base. This land, as well as that of private citizens, was purchased through intermediaries of the Commercial Club and donated to the US government. The image above shows a deed transferring the property of Brigette and Edward Fitzgerald to Adolphus C. Bartlett, Charles L. Hutchinson, and John J. Janes, representative of the Commercial Club.

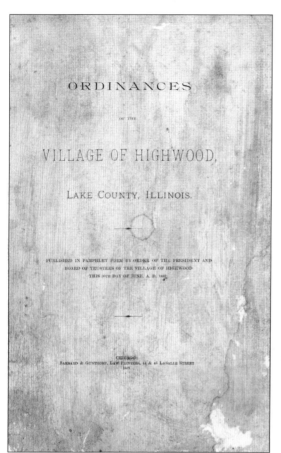

ORDINANCES

OF THE

VILLAGE OF HIGHWOOD,

LAKE COUNTY, ILLINOIS.

PUBLISHED IN PAMPHLET FORM BY ORDER OF THE PRESIDENT AND
BOARD OF TRUSTEES OF THE VILLAGE OF HIGHWOOD
THIS 30TH DAY OF JUNE, A. D, 1887.

CHICAGO:
BARNARD & GUNTHORP, LAW PRINTERS, 44 & 46 LASALLE STREET
1887.

In 1887, the neighboring village of Highwood was incorporated. Ole Onsom was elected board president. Andrew Wahlman, John Garrity, and William F. Hogan were the first trustees. Just one year later, perhaps hoping to latch onto the allure of the parading cavalry, the village changed its name to Fort Sheridan.

The Village of Fort Sheridan completed work on a new village hall in 1898. The council chamber was located on the second floor, occupying the entire east half. The clerk's office was in the southwest corner of the building. The jail room, with four cells, was situated on the north side of the first floor. Although taken at a later date, this picture depicts this building.

CITY HALL HIGHWOOD ILL. H 3

This picture shows the trustees of the village of Fort Sheridan in about 1902. From left to right are (first row) Charles Roberg, James Reilly, and John Brady; (second row) unidentified, City Judge Cummings, village president William F. Hogan, and Solomon Savage; (third row) John Condon, H. Swanson, Charles Benson, E. Carlson, Dan Brady, Ed Welch, and Charles Gordon. Hogan was a carpenter by trade and built homes during Highwood's infancy. As well as being involved in the city's government, he was a realtor and saloon keeper. He also owned a meeting site called Hogan's Hall. Welch would become involved in the saloon business. The Peter Shoenhoffer Brewing Company would provide a mortgage to Benson, thus cementing the village's early identity as a saloon town.

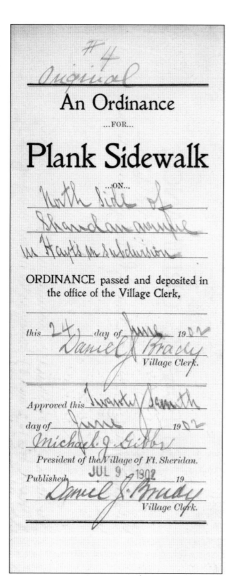

# An Ordinance

## ...FOR...

# Plank Sidewalk

### ...ON...

*North Side of*
*Sheridan avenue*
*in Hart's Subdivision*

ORDINANCE passed and deposited in
the office of the Village Clerk,

this _24_ day of _June_ 19_02_

*Daniel J. Brady*

Village Clerk.

Approved this *Twenty Seventh*

day of _June_ 19_02_

*Michael J. Gibb*

President of the Village of Ft. Sheridan.

Published JUL 9 1902 19___

*Daniel J. Brady*

Village Clerk.

The incorporation of the village of Fort Sheridan
and its later change to a city created a need for
continued municipal improvements. For example,
the picture to the left shows an ordinance that
was passed in 1902 by the village to build a plank
sidewalk on Sheridan Avenue in the residential
district. Within four years, continuing population
growth created an urgent need for improvements
on a far grander scale. In August 1906, at a special
meeting, the city council passed an ordinance
for the construction of two miles of cement
sidewalks. In addition, ordinances were passed
for the extension of water mains including the
laying of water mains in several side streets. The
picture below shows a funding bond for the
City of Highwood, paid on August 10, 1909.

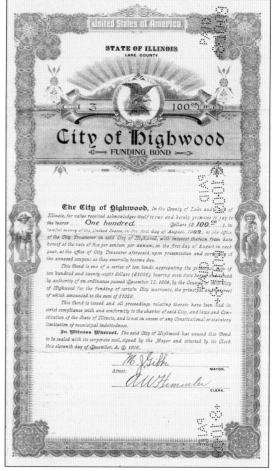

The new village hall also housed the fire department's equipment. Pictured here is the fire department in the early 1900s. The city of Highland Park's fire department was often called on to answer fire calls in Highwood. According to the *Highland Park Press* newspaper of March 18, 1920, an ordinance was prepared by the City of Highwood to be passed in April for the issuance of corporate bonds in the amount of $3,000 for the purchase of a new Ford-Howe fire truck. This vehicle would be similar to one that had recently been purchased by Highland Park. Volunteer firemen made up the staff of the Highwood Fire Department, and it remained a volunteer force until 1980. The picture below shows members of the department in 1935. Depicted are Fred "Dutch" Kehrwald, Albert Lyle, Ed Kehrwald, and Art Kehrwald.

The postcard depicts the Chicago & North Western Railway station, which is located in the heart of Highwood's business district. Since its inception in the 1850s, the railroad has always played an important role in the growth and development of the North Shore. The railroad also featured significantly in the initial transportation of troops to the future Fort Sheridan military post. Another station was built about a mile north to serve Fort Sheridan.

**HIGHWOOD – CAR BARNS AND SHOPS**

The Bluff City Electric Street Railway Company had already extended south from Waukegan through the village of Fort Sheridan by 1898 when a five-acre site on the village's north end was selected as the rail line's headquarters. Barns, a powerhouse, and administrative offices followed. The rail line, acquired in 1916 by Samuel Insull, became known as the Chicago, North Shore & Milwaukee Road and, later, the North Shore Line.

The North Shore Railroad line ran parallel to that of the Chicago & North Western Railway through the town of Highwood. Shown in the picture above is the North Shore track in the foreground with the North Western track and train station in the background. Another North Shore station was several blocks to the north on Washington Avenue, serving the Fort Sheridan Amusement Park with an entrance on the same street.

The image is that of a North Shore Line pin-on button that was probably worn by some railroad employees. It is currently on display in the Highwood Historical Society Museum in Highwood, Illinois. The button is a reminder to the community of the importance the railway had in terms of jobs for Highwood citizens as well as the ease of transportation in and out of town for its residents and visitors.

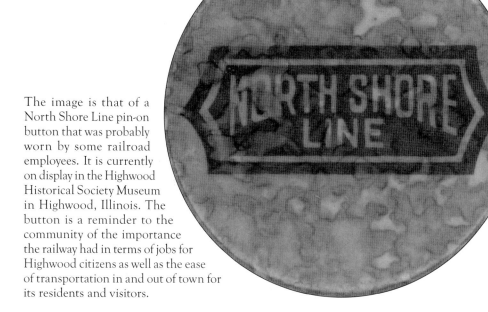

Fort Sheridan Park, a 10-acre amusement park, was located at the corner of Clay Street and Waukegan Avenue. Cars of the Chicago & Milwaukee Electric Railway would stop at Washington Avenue, one-half block from the park's entrance. The pavilion, shown here, provided theater and dancing, vaudeville acts, concerts, and vocalists. A program on Christmas Day 1899 was expected to draw over 300 children, with Santa Claus distributing gifts of fruits and confections.

The Fort Sheridan Hotel (later named the Park Hotel) was located across the street from the Fort Sheridan Amusement Park at Clay Street and Washington Avenue. In May 1899, newspaper accounts stated that the hotel was newly decorated due to the expected increase in summer patronage. The "artistic decorating" was performed by W.P. Rutherford, a painter and decorator from Highwood.

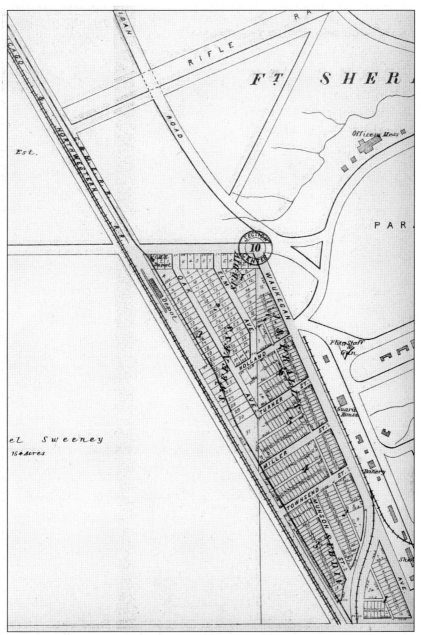

The village of Fort Sheridan became the city of Highwood in 1904. Two years later, the federal government obtained the northeast corner of town, including Fort Sheridan Park. Lots in J.S. Prall's Fort Sheridan subdivision, a small subdivision to the north that had been recently added to the city of Highwood, were also purchased. In this picture, the platted streets and lots are visible on the left portion of the map. These purchases reduced the size of Highwood significantly. Numerous families were displaced, but many moved to other locations in Highwood. This area was later referred to as "the Forgotten Village" and described by a former resident, Ruth Rettig Reilly. Some of these properties were not developed but owned by prominent men in the area and beyond, including Frank P. Hawkins, former mayor of Highland Park, and William F. Hogan of Highwood. A most interesting owner was Gustav Pabst of the Pabst Brewing Company.

The building shown above was Highwood's first grade school and was thought to be erected in 1876. A later addition to the west side expanded the school to six classrooms. In early 1916, after an inspection by the state, the building was condemned. Highwood was required to provide another building within two years and had one year to raise funds for a new school at a different location. As of this writing, the building still stands at the corner of High Street and Prairie Avenue. Some of the early students at Highwood's first school came from the Curley, Fagan, Mahonan, Frank, Stupey, Summers, Garrity, and Mowers families. Two of the early teachers were Miss Wheeler and Philip O'Mahoney.

On August 12, 1916, approval was given to purchase the Pease property across the street from the original school. Bonds in the amount of $20,000 were issued to pay for the project. Construction began in the fall of 1916, and the new school was finished in the summer of 1917. It was named Oak Terrace School. The image below depicts students in their classroom around 1924. Some of the families represented are Watson, Walsh, Griese, Curley, and Ori. The Curley family dates back to the founding of Highwood. Students from Fort Sheridan also attended Oak Terrace.

St James Catholic Church
Highwood Ill. Sep 8. 1912

These photographs are of St. James Church, located at the corner of North and Funston Avenues. The church was dedicated by Archbishop James E. Quigley on September 8, 1912. It served not only Highwood but also the soldiers of Fort Sheridan. Later, a bell tower was constructed at the front of the church. This addition also served to protect the front steps from the elements. After a new church was built farther to the east, the old church was used as a church hall and kindergarten for St. James School. The school provided a choice for Fort Sheridan residents who wanted their children to attend a private school.

# *Two*

# GROWING TOGETHER

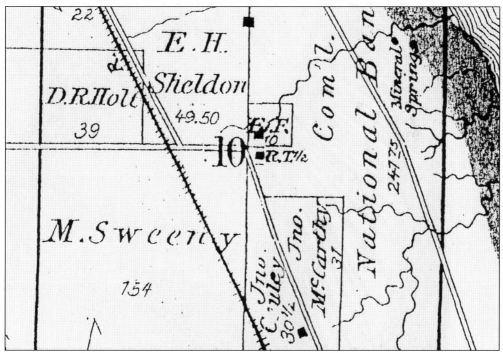

Even before 1887, when Highwood was incorporated as a village and Camp Highwood was established as a military post, Highwood and the Army began their relationship. Most of the land was purchased from banks, but several smaller tracts owned by E.H. Sheldon, Daniel A. Jones, John McCarthy, and Edward Fitzgerald were also acquired. Some, like Edward Fitzgerald, bought lots and moved to Highwood, leaving farming for other occupations.

Arriving by rail on November 8, 1887, eighty soldiers of Companies F and K, 6th Infantry Regiment, US Army, commanded by Maj. William J. Lyster, disembarked at Highwood, Illinois. What lay before them were acres of uncleared land. These first troops lived in tents until 1889, when Congress approved the construction of permanent buildings.

Civilian labor was needed to help build accommodations for six companies of infantry and four troops of cavalry, a water tower, a wharf, a cemetery, and a rifle range. Scores of laborers came to work at Fort Sheridan, many traveling to and from Chicago. Herman Swanson, Herbert Nafe, and Mr. Nevins are pictured here among various workmen at Fort Sheridan. Construction materials were brought to the site by the Chicago & North Western spur track.

The Fort Sheridan Water Tower and Barracks, built from 1889 to 1891, was one of the first structures completed in the fort. Inspired by St. Mark's Campanile in Venice, it was built with cream-colored bricks made from lake bluff clay and topped with a red terra cotta roof. The water tower has long been the iconic landmark of Fort Sheridan. It is listed in the National Register of Historic Places.

Clay from the bluffs along the shores of Lake Michigan near Fort Sheridan was used to make the brick for the construction of the 66 buildings designed by Holabird and Roche and 26 buildings from standardized plans from the Office of the Quartermaster General. All the buildings were constructed between 1889 and 1908 using the same cream-colored brick, which was made at the fort.

Employment opportunities continued to draw people to the Highwood area. Some came to lay tracks for the Bluff City Electric Company, an existing Waukegan street railroad. In time, the railroad bought out the small railroad running through Fort Sheridan, Highwood, and Highland Park. By August 1899, Bluff City Electric Company had extended rail service from downtown Waukegan to Church Street in Evanston.

Others came to work at Fort Sheridan as additional acres and a larger garrison were added to the post. Beyond construction, civilians were employed in almost all areas of the fort such as the laundry pictured here. With the assurance of steady employment and affordable housing, workmen began to settle in Highwood to raise their families, and by 1900, the population of Highwood had grown to 1,219.

Julius C. Laegeler came to the United States from Germany in 1883, serving in the Army as a hospital steward. After his tour of duty at Fort Sheridan ended in 1891, Mr. Barrett and Julius Laegeler opened the first pharmacy in Highwood near the corner of Highwood and Waukegan Avenues. Julius married Sarah Unbehaun that same year. When Julius became the sole owner, he moved his business and opened the Enterprise Drug Company. Julius is shown above on the far right in about 1899 in front of his store, where his father-in-law Unbehaun's butcher shop had been. He later moved his business across the street to the northeast corner of Highwood and Waukegan Avenues, as shown below. Note the sign above the entrance reading "Apotheke," the German word for "apothecary" or "drugstore."

The building housing the newly located Laegeler business had served earlier as the site of the general store owned by Samuel Breakwell. Sarah Laegeler, shown to the left outside of the drugstore, kept the business open after her husband's sudden death in 1913 by hiring pharmacists until her sons received their pharmacy degrees. Laegeler's Pharmacy closed in 2000 after 109 years. It is one of the oldest Highwood businesses to date continuously operated by the same family. The Breakwell building was torn down in 1927 to make way for a new Laegeler's Pharmacy building at the corner of Highwood and Waukegan Avenues, as seen below.

With the influx of soldiers and workmen at Fort Sheridan, neighboring Highwood quickly gained a reputation as a tavern town. In 1893, the village approved liquor licensing, hoping to end illegal "blind pigs" and the problems they brought. By 1900, Highwood had 13 saloons. Pictured here on Waukegan Avenue, Highwood, from left to right, are unknown; Ed Welch's bowling alley; John Goehringer's The Edelweiss saloon; the Highwood Buffet, managed by Herman Reichardt; and John Garrity's grocery–meat market.

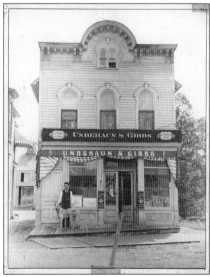

Michael Gibbs and Charlie Unbehaun operated the Unbehaun & Gibbs tavern and grocery store on Waukegan Avenue. Gibbs began his political career as the first fire marshal and then the first mayor of the city of Fort Sheridan. In 1904, he became the first mayor of the city of Highwood when the city name reverted to "Highwood." Gibbs also served as chief of police, health inspector, and postmaster before his death in 1935.

Vencel Muzik was transferred to Fort Sheridan from Fort Snelling, Minnesota, in 1887 to work on the new fort. He married Catherine Hickey in 1895. After his army discharge, in 1896 he opened Muzik's store on Waukegan Avenue, pictured here. Muzik sold that business when he was called to duty in the Spanish-American War. He came home in 1898 to "Muzik's Mansion," his large house on Railway Avenue in the center of town. Many guests and events were hosted there. Soldiers and their families were welcomed to stay until jobs and housing could be found. Fund-raisers were held in their huge yard. Some monies raised were used to build St. James Catholic Church. Catholic settlers attended religious services at Fort Sheridan until 1907. Mass was then celebrated in Highwood's city hall on Waukegan Avenue by a mission pastor until St. James was built in 1912.

The Santi brothers, shown here in 1911, operated a bakery and grocery store. Brothers Frank (left) and Sante (right) started in Highwood in 1906 in the building later occupied by Innocenzi Grocery and Market. By 1915, they opened Santi Brothers Groceries & Bakery in their new building on the northwest corner of Railway and Highwood Avenues. Business thrived as they sold meat and groceries to the Fort Sheridan commissary.

Pasquale "Pat" and Josephine Innocenzi purchased the Santi bakery building on Waukegan Avenue in 1921 and opened Innocenzi's Grocery and Market, which they ran until they retired in 1943. Like the Santi brothers, the Innocenzis' business was successful in part due to their sales to Fort Sheridan. Leonard Innocenzi, their grandson, owns Buffo's Restaurant, located in the old Innocenzi Grocery and Market building. The restaurant celebrated its 45th anniversary in 2022.

Pictured here is the military funeral of Cpl. Eugene G. Miller, a soldier in Company B, US 5th Cavalry, at Fort Sheridan, overseen by veterans of the Spanish-American War and Auxiliary. The funeral services were held on Sunday afternoon, February 27, 1916, at the War Veterans' Hall in Highwood, Illinois.

Following the military services at the War Veterans' Hall, a funeral procession proceeded on foot through town to St. James Catholic Church, North Avenue, Highwood, where Fr. S.J. Gates officiated at Cpl. Eugene G. Miller's funeral mass. Even though a chapel was available at Fort Sheridan, the services were held in town.

The funeral procession resumed for another two miles from the church to Fort Sheridan Post Cemetery, with the deceased's horse, which the corporal had ridden for many years, following immediately behind the coffin, empty-saddled. There, the flag-draped casket on a horse-drawn limber and caisson was met by B Troop and the band.

Representatives from nearly all the military camps and auxiliaries in the Chicago area were present. Miller was buried with all possible military honors, including an honor guard, folding and presentation of the US flag, sounding of "Taps," firing of volley shots as a salute, and other military elements.

MILITARY FUNERAL
EUGENE G. MILLER FEB 27 1916
FORT SHERIDAN ILL.

CORPL.
EUGENE G. MILLER
CO.B.
5 U.S.CAV.

In memoriam, John B. Matthews, Company B, wrote, "Of our beloved comrade, Corporal Eugene G. Miller. From our ranks a comrade missing. We no more his face shall see. 'Til we answer to the roll call of that final reveille. When life's battle, it is over, and the trumpets cease to call. As we climb the golden staircase to the great ethereal hall. There to face, the great tribunal. Free from every earthly care. Where life's efforts are rewarded. We shall find him waiting there. Ever faithful to his duty and gifted with a sunny disposition, he was esteemed by all who knew him, and his memory will ever linger with us." Eugene G. Miller is one of many Army veterans interred at Fort Sheridan Post Cemetery. The cemetery was established in 1889. Veterans of conflicts from the Civil War to the present times are interred there.

*Officers Training Camp.* 7/2/17

Pictured here is the Fort Sheridan Officers' Training Camp (OTC) on July 2, 1917, in the municipal park at the intersection of Waukegan Avenue and Highwood Avenue in downtown Highwood. The small building in the background is the old North Shore Streetcar Station. As early as 1910, Maj. Gen. Leonard Wood believed that the citizen soldier should be trained as a stand-by force prepared for deployment in case of war. The first of two Reserve Officers' Training Camps at Fort Sheridan was held from May 15 to August 15, 1917. The camps trained more than 5,000 men as officers in the Army Reserves upon completion of three months of basic training. The Declaration of War on April 6, 1917, caused Fort Sheridan to transition from OTC camps to an induction and Midwest training center for Army recruits from Illinois, Michigan, and Wisconsin.

The bronze plaque on Building 38 reads, "Originally constructed as a Veterinarian Hospital, 1890," but records indicate that the original purpose was quartermaster stables. Patrick Hickey knew these stables and the nearby blacksmith shops well. He immigrated to the United States from Ireland in 1876 and began his Army career shoeing horses. Hickey brought his family to Highwood following a two-year deployment in Cuba. He was a farrier for 47 years, with 19 spent at Fort Sheridan's post blacksmith shop. Patrick's son James Hickey Sr. also served in the Army in World War I and worked at Fort Sheridan in the finance department. His grandson James Jr. served in World War II, was a prisoner of war in Germany for a short time, and was awarded the Purple Heart.

By the late 1890s, horses were valued as much by civilians as they were by the military. Horse-drawn wagons and buggies were the modes of transportation, as shown here in front of Fritsch Bros. Grocery Store, owned by Clinton and Ben Fritsch. So Fort Sheridan horse sales drew buyers from all over the region looking for a bargain. Horses considered overage for military duty were still useful for other work, and several local businessmen purchased horses for as little as $10, including Albert Shelton, the Highwood milkman. Within days, Shelton's new steed, hearing the call to assembly, ignored the milkman and raced into line with the other mounts. His unfortunate and comical story is well known and served as a lesson for others thinking of buying horses at the sale. Also pictured are the village harness maker, M.J. Hook, and his daughter. Hook lived in nearby Highland Park

From the beginning, Highwood wanted to capitalize on the glamour of the cavalrymen and, in 1888, voted to change Highwood's name to the village of Fort Sheridan only one year after its incorporation. By 1904, however, the city decided to revert to its original title of Highwood due to residents' mounting frustration with postal misrouting and railroad stop confusion. Four cavalry units—the 7th Cavalry (Troops B and K) in 1891, the 3rd Cavalry (Troop B) in 1900, the 15th Cavalry (3rd Squadron) in 1908, and the 5th Cavalry in 1916—were activated at Fort Sheridan before the 14th Cavalry arrived in 1920. The 14th Cavalry would be the last. World War I introduced mechanized vehicles to the battlefield. Soon, the days of horse-drawn artillery and cavalry would end. Horses would be replaced with automobiles, tanks, and trucks, and the all-purpose mechanic would replace blacksmiths, wheelwrights, and wagon masters.

Highwood shared the nation's economic boom of the 1920s. Job opportunities brought a wave of Italian immigrants to the North Shore to work on the great estates and country clubs in Lake Forest and Highland Park. Many were construction laborers, and some opened their own businesses. Highwood's population more than doubled from 1,446 in 1920 to 3,590 in 1930. Pictured are construction workers at the Highwood Disposal Plant built in 1922.

The Gandolfi Grocery and Market, pictured around 1929, was owned and operated by Mary and Atilio Gandolfi. First named Moraine Grocery, it was located on Railway Avenue (now Green Bay Road). Mary continued to live above and operate the store after her husband's death in 1942 and worked into her later years making and selling tortellini. Mary Gandolfi died in 1999 at the age of 94 and is considered one of Highwood's longest-living business owners.

In the early 1920s, twice-widowed Linda Bosselli Pigati came to Highwood from a Southern Illinois mining town with her three sons in tow. She married Billy Biagetti in 1927, and in 1933, they purchased the Del Rio Grill from Silvio and Nina Muzzarelli, using the $500 bonus issued by President Roosevelt to World War I veterans during the Depression to stimulate the economy. The Del Rio, a fine-dining northern Italian restaurant, is one of the oldest family-owned businesses in Highwood. It has remained in the same location at 228 Green Bay Road for close to a century, passing down from generation to generation and still welcoming diners today. The restaurant was named for Dolores Del Rio, the famous Latin American actress considered to be one of the most beautiful women in Hollywood in the 1920s.

The Highwood Civic Improvement Association was formed in 1926 to promote community progress and civic cooperation. Monies raised at annual Highwood Days celebrations (as pictured), carnivals, and parades were used to support Boy Scout troops and other youth groups, purchase equipment for Oak Terrace School, and sponsor a band that played in the park at the corner of Highwood and Waukegan Avenues. The 14th Cavalry horse show monies were also contributed to support Oak Terrace School.

In 1927, Highwood Days were held on Labor Day weekend. Saturday night featured games, dancing, and music by the Blue Bird orchestra at Fort Sheridan Park. Monday's parade kicked off at 1:00 p.m. The Fort Sheridan band, which often participated in Highwood events, is shown proceeding south on Railway Avenue, now Green Bay Road, along the parade route under the viaduct and then north on Waukegan Avenue to Fort Sheridan Park.

Decorated silk objects with patriotic and military themes became very popular with World War I soldiers wanting to purchase a remembrance of their service. By World War II, many souvenirs were produced for specific military bases, such as this vintage World War II souvenir pillow with fringe for US Army Fort Sheridan, Illinois. Colorfully printed on silk-like fabrics often edged with fringe, they depicted battle scenes, equipment, and post buildings.

Also popular in the early 1900s were picture postcards. More than a convenient way for people to communicate, they provided a snapshot of American life and were produced for every occasion. This World War II "Greetings from Fort Sheridan, Illinois," postcard shows a gas mask drill (S), service club (H), barracks (E), entrance (R), the tower (I), officers' club (D), chapel (A), and the colors pass in review (N).

# Three

# THE FORT, CAVALRY OFFICERS, AND RECRUITS

This is an early view of Fort Sheridan looking east from Highwood to Lake Michigan. The most dominant structure shown is the 1891 water tower complex, consisting of a 227-foot-high water tower with barracks on each side. An access road runs north through the "sally port" brick arch of the water tower. This early "horse and buggy" road was eliminated when motorized vehicles were unable to pass through safely. The main gates are near Sheridan Road welcoming numerous US presidents and worldwide guests. Many soldiers settled in Highwood after their discharge.

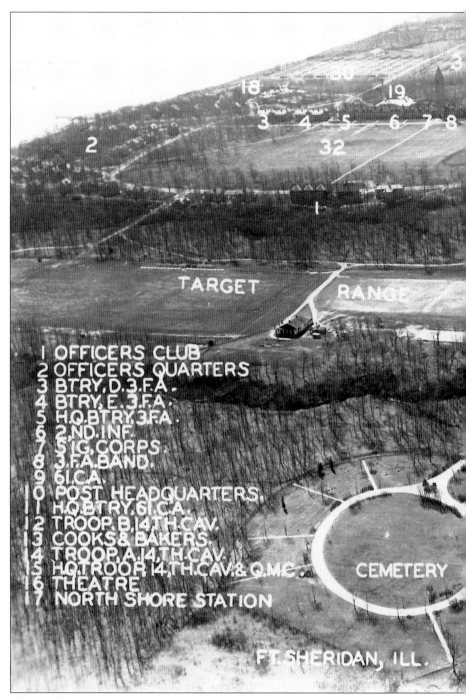

1 OFFICERS CLUB
2 OFFICERS QUARTERS
3 BTRY. D. 3. F.A.
4 BTRY. E. 3. F.A.
5 H.Q. BTRY 3 F.A.
6 2.ND. INF.
7 SIG. CORPS.
8 3. F.A. BAND.
9 61. C.A.
10 POST HEADQUARTERS.
11 H.Q. BTRY. 61. C.A.
12 TROOP. B. 14TH. CAV.
13 COOKS & BAKERS.
14 TROOP. A. 14. TH. CAV.
15 H.Q. TROOP 14. TH. CAV. & Q.MC.
16 THEATRE
17 NORTH SHORE STATION

TARGET RANGE

CEMETERY

FT. SHERIDAN, ILL.

This 1930s aerial view of Fort Sheridan, taken from the north, shows the post cemetery, shaped like a wagon wheel with 10 spokes dividing the sections and a large grassy round hub in the center. Established in 1889, the first internment was Sgt. Edward Quinn, who died on October 5, 1890. In December 2019, the cemetery was designated a national cemetery when the US Veterans Administration took control of it. Prior to this, Lake Country Forest Preserve maintained it. Next is the target range it was converted to an airstrip in the 1950s. The airstrip is gone, and a natural

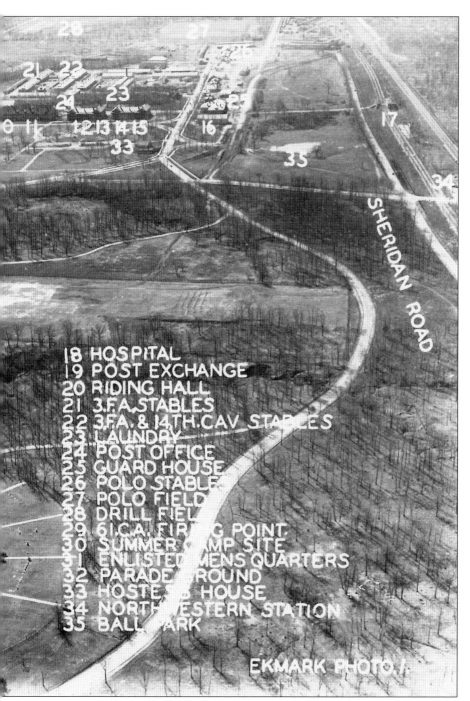

18 HOSPITAL
19 POST EXCHANGE
20 RIDING HALL
21 3.F.A. STABLES
22 3.F.A. & 14TH. CAV. STABLES
23 LAUNDRY
24 POST OFFICE
25 GUARD HOUSE
26 POLO STABLE
27 POLO FIELD
28 DRILL FIELD
29 61.C.A. FIRING POINT
30 SUMMER CAMP SITE
31 ENLISTED MENS QUARTERS
32 PARADE GROUND
33 HOSTESS HOUSE
34 NORTHWESTERN STATION
35 BALL PARK

SHERIDAN ROAD

EKMARK PHOTO.

savanna of oak trees has been allowed to mature. The parade grounds are south of the Officers' Club and their quarters. To the east of the parade grounds are the Post Headquarters, the 14th Cavalry, Signal Corps, and Army Band Headquarters. The Cook and Bakers Building is grouped with the 14th Cavalry and Hostess House. Farther south is the cavalry riding hall, barracks, and stables. The drill field is the farthest south. The entire fort evokes a sense of old Army post traditions and contributes strong values to US military history.

Here lies Army first sergeant, 7th Cavalry, John Hackett (1851–1904) at Fort Sheridan Post Cemetery. He was one of four soldiers buried here serving under Lt. Col. George Armstrong Custer during the Little Big Horn Indian War in Montana Territory. During the 1876 battle, Hackett retreated wounded from an earlier valley skirmish to a hill and survived. After discharge, he settled in Highwood, working at the fort's hospital. In 1902, he married Esther Smith, a laundress at the fort. John Hackett was a fireman in Highwood until his death.

"Thoughts from Fort Sheridan" was a 1930s photograph available for purchase at the fort's commissary. Many soldiers believed it was a good description of their days in the Army. The last sentence seems to conclude their views of how tough it could be. The author is unidentified, except for the initials of J.D.S. appearing in the lower right corner.

*Thoughts from Fort Sheridan*

I'm sitting here thinking of the things I left behind,
And I'd hate to put on paper what's runnin thru my mind.
We've dug a million ditches and cleared ten miles of ground,
And a meaner place this side of Hell is waiting to be found.
But there is one consolation - gather closely while I tell,
When we die we'll go to Heaven, for we've done our hitch in Hell.

We've built a hundred kitchens for the cooks to stew our beans
Stood a million guard-mounts and cleaned the camp latrines,
Washed a million dishes and peeled a million spuds,
Rolled a million blanket rolls and washed our Captain's duds.
The number of parade we've stood is very hard to tell,
We won't have to parade in Heaven for we've done our hitch in Hell.

We've killed a million rats and bugs that cried out for our oats,
And shook a million pounds of sand out of our dirty sheets,
We've marched a million miles and made a million camps,
And we've pulled a million sanburs from the seat of our pants,
But when our work is done on earth, our friends behind will tell,
When they died they went to Heaven, for they'd done their hitch in Hell.

When finally taps is sounded and we lay aside our troubles and cares,
we will do our last parade up those shining Golden Stairs,
The angels all will welcome us and harps will start to play,
We will draw a million canteen books and spend them in a day,
It is then we'll hear St.Peter tell us loudly with a yell,
Take a front seat boys, for you've done your hitch in Hell.

J.D.S.

A 1930s aerial view taken from the post water tower looks south at the stables, riding hall, and drill field. In 1949, a structural problem with the tower necessitated the reconstruction of the conical roof, reducing the tower's height from 227 feet to 169 feet. The fort in general exemplifies the importance of the horse and mule to the Army, the separation of rank, and the growing attention paid to the needs of the soldier connected with military life.

The Chicago & North Western Railway steam engine No. 1450 is seen leaving the depot at Highwood. The train is heading north passing the fort's barracks and stables in the background. The railroad was the most important transportation entity in America and to Fort Sheridan. This railway line provided transportation for passengers and goods from Chicago to Milwaukee, Wisconsin, and beyond. Railroads during this time were operating with riskiness after the 1929 stock market crash.

These are the 1930s commanding officers at Fort Sheridan: from left to right, chief of staff Maj. Gen. Charles Summerall, Maj. Gen. Frank Parker, and Col. Robert John Binford. Binford was born in Indiana in 1879. He enlisted in the US Army in 1899 and served in the Philippine Islands and Belgium. Binford's last post was Fort Sheridan after 30 years of service, and his retirement came on March 31, 1933, as a colonel. He was interred at Fort Rosecrans National Cemetery, San Diego, California, in May 1953.

The 14th Cavalry Regiment is in a review drill practice at Fort Sheridan parade grounds. Horses in the 1930s were vital to the cavalry. Most people think the cavalry disbanded after Lieutenant Colonel Custer and his troops were defeated, but the cavalry carried on for about 66 more years. The mounted cavalry lasted until 1942, when horses were replaced by motorized units, ending the Army's exclusive use of the equine.

It would be unjust to conclude that in peacetime the cavalry was doing nothing. On the contrary, they were very active and had a strong sense of mission. All the cavalry troops were involved in military training, equestrian competitions, ceremonial events, escort duties, and maintaining public order. Pictured here is the 14th Cavalry Regiment on command practicing with sabers in an attack mode on the drill field at Fort Sheridan. The cavalrymen had to control their horses after they mastered marching, command formations, and basic use of weapons. The US Cavalry regiment was the most expensive soldier to maintain, and the military assigned the best available horses and equipment to them.

A.T.R. TOP KICK.

Maj. Gen. Charles Pelo Summerall (1867–1955) was a senior US Army officer. He graduated from Porter Military Academy in South Carolina. Summerall attended West Point Military Academy and graduated in June 1892. He served on the front line in France during World War I. Summerall was commander of the 1st Division and later became commander of the 5th Corps. In 1926, he became chief of staff of the US Army, and he was later promoted to full four-star general in 1929. In November 1930, after 38 years of service, he retired from the US Army after his last assignment at Fort Sheridan. In 1931, Summerall took a position as president of the Citadel, where he stayed for 22 years, retiring in 1953. He died in Washington, DC, in 1954 and rests at the Arlington National Cemetery with his wife, Laura (Mordecai) Summerall.

Maj. Gen. Frank C. Parker (1872–1947) was in the US Army at Fort Sheridan. His awards include the Army Distinguished Service Medal, two Silver Star Citations, and numerous foreign decorations and civilian accolades. In 1904, Parker graduated from the Cavalry School in Saumur, France. He served as military attaché in Caracas, Venezuela, from 1904 to 1905, in Buenos Aires, Argentina, from 1905 to 1906, and in Cuba from 1906 to 1908. He was an instructor and organizer of the cavalry in Cuba from 1909 to 1912. In 1912, Parker attended the École Supérieure de Guerre, France. After his retirement on September 30, 1936, Parker made his home in Chicago. He served as the executive director of the Illinois War Council during World War II. He died on March 13, 1947, in Chicago, Illinois, and was buried at Mansfield Cemetery in Mansfield, Ohio.

Capt. Wade Carpenter Gatchell (1895–1995) of 14th Cavalry, Company B, sits on his big white horse named Jack. Gatchell served in the Army from 1916 to 1946 and retired in 1946 as colonel. After graduating from Norwich University, Northfield, Vermont, he entered the US Army as a second lieutenant. He was eventually assigned to the 6th Cavalry and participated in World War I, serving with his father, Brig. Gen. George W. Gatchell. After World War I, Gatchell was assigned and served at numerous posts, which included the 1st Cavalry at Camp Marfa, Texas, and Fort Sheridan, Illinois, and the 14th Cavalry at the onset of World War II. Gatchell was first with the 6th Armored Division at Fort Knox and later joined the 10th Armored Division at Cherbourg, France. He was assigned to Patton's 3rd Army. Gatchell was a 10th Armored commander during the Battle of the Bulge. He easily can be spotted throughout the troop photographs in parades and on-field hikes riding his white horse Jack. Gatchell is interred at Greenwood Memorials Park Cemetery in San Diego, California.

Shown are nine officers of the more than twenty that were in charge at Fort Sheridan in the 1930s. Most of them are riding American Quarter Horses. The only officer identified is Capt. Wade Carpenter Gatchell on his big white horse named Jack, also a Quarter Horse. The white variety is the very rarest of that breed. Officers were responsible for the well-being of their horses, as were the enlisted soldiers. The cavalry regiments are organized as follows: each regiment consisted of 12 troops, composed of approximately 100 men, with a first lieutenant, a second lieutenant, and a supernumerary lieutenant. In addition, the fort's commanding officers were the ranks general, major general, and colonel.

Pictured here is 14th Cavalry, Company B, at Fort Sheridan on January 30, 1931. They are listed as (first row) Sgt. Gilbert Olson (47), Norway; Sgt. John Rutkowski (26), Poland; Sgt. Baldwin; 1st Sgt. Joseph Espinola (38), Spain; 1st Lt. John Bethel (35), Washington; Capt. Wade C. Gatchell (35), Vermont; Lt. Prentice Yeomans (28), New York; Sgt. Anton Martinkus (22), Greece; Sgt. Grover Squires (45), Wisconsin; Sgt. Frank Kloss (41), Germany; and mascots Schnapps and Buster; (second row) Herald Herbert (21), Michigan; Edw. Celichowski (28), Illinois; Robert Baker (34), Kentucky; Anthony Lang (19), Illinois; Cpl. Fred Van Berkum (36), New Jersey; Cpl. James Kerwin (24), Missouri; Cpl. William Harris (19), Ohio; Cpl. Steve Domitrom (35), Russia; Cpl. Gust Rusis (26), Greece; Cpl. Hartland Burbank (19), Michigan; Corporal Keerns; Cpl. James C. Curwood (25), New York; Cpl. Gilbert Olson (47), Norway; Eric Banfield (19), England; Potts; Theodore Zabrisky (23), Wisconsin; and Cpl. William H. Herman (27), Wisconsin; (third row)

John D. Duresa (19), Illinois; Edward Arneson (19), North Dakota; Alton Garlick (18), Michigan; Mack; Dave Sagel (26), Russia; Hicks; Louis Koski (36), Poland; George Milam (19), South Dakota; Melvin Pultz (21), Virginia; William Custer (21), Illinois; Saveressig; Joseph Wazlow (22), Illinois; Daniel Schmucker (23), Illinois; William Damber (29), Russia; Harry Wallace (19), Illinois; Leon Saunders (19), Michigan; and Kmiecik; (fourth row) Brown; Wilbur Manchester (18), Michigan; Gilbert Peat (18), Illinois; Paul S. Wieland (24), Indiana; Kulikowski; Szychulski; Charles Conrad (19), West Virginia; Harvey Hunt (24), Montana; Schmick; Davidson; Robert V. Watton (41), Illinois; James Collins (30), Missouri; Joel Boudreaux (20), Louisiana; Karl Meyer (24), Germany; Leonard Simonis (19), Wisconsin; Austin Keeley (23), Connecticut; Edward Brandt (23), South Dakota; Robert Bell (20), Michigan; Van Wagner; and Scholtz.

At enlistment in 1930, Pvt. John D. Duresa was assigned to the 14th Cavalry, Company B. Duresa is in front of the stables at the fort, riding a newly trained horse. A Quarter Horse was the preferred warhorse for the US Army. At 18 years old, Duresa's job was to break and train the horses for warfare. He also trained mules to pull wagons. Replacement of these animals was an ongoing process and vital to the US Cavalry of the 1930s and 1940s.

Pvt. John Duresa is riding on a box wagon with the 14th Cavalry's mascot Buster. Wagons carried artillery, and during camping trips, they held field supplies. Troops and artillery had priority of movement on the march, while ammunition wagons took precedence over the supply wagons. Keeping wagons rolling was the duty of the staff of every Army post. For this reason, box wagons were considered the workhorse of a regiment.

Troop B of the 14th Cavalry is sitting on the stairs of the fort barracks with mascots Buster and Schnapps. Pvt. John Duresa is pictured in the first row, third from the left, with 26 other soldiers. This group of cavalrymen have gone through over 20 weeks of training and are considered the elite soldiers of their time. Some of the training took place in the classroom, but it mostly involved horsemanship in field practice. Whether it was taking part in troop field maneuvers, target practice, or war games, cavalrymen were constantly refining their skills to keep themselves sharp. The 14th Cavalry was also known for contributing to and competing in horse shows and polo games at the fort. Back in the 1930s, it was the order of the day that horses first, men second, and then the trooper's equipment were all to be taken care of before any soldier's leisure time. Most of these young men considered themselves fortunate to have a roof over their heads and three square meals a day, since this was during the Great Depression, when jobs were impossible to find.

# Honorable Discharge

from

# The Army of the United States

## TO ALL WHOM IT MAY CONCERN:

**This is to Certify,** That* _John D. Duresa_

† _6,805,094 Private Troop "B" 14th Cavalry_

THE ARMY OF THE UNITED STATES, as a TESTIMONIAL OF HONEST
AND FAITHFUL SERVICE, is hereby HONORABLY DISCHARGED from the
military service of the UNITED STATES by reason of ‡ _Expiration_
_Term of Service_

Said _John D Duresa_ was born
in _Chicago_, in the State of _Illinois_
When enlisted he was _19-4_ years of age and by occupation a _Machinist Help_
He had _Blue_ eyes, _Blonde_ hair, _Fair_ complexion, and
was _5_ feet _6 ¾_ inches in height.

Given under my hand at _Fort Sheridan, Illinois_ this
_14th_ day of _June_, one thousand nine hundred and ~~twenty~~ _thirty three_

_C.C. Stuitt_

_Major 14th Cavalry_

Commanding.

See A R. 345–470.
*Insert name; as, "John J. Doe."
† Insert Army serial number, grade, company, regiment, and branch; as "1620302"; "Corporal, Company A, 1st Infantry"; "Sergeant, Quartermaster Corps."
‡ If discharged prior to expiration of service, give number, date, and source of order or full description of authority therefor.

W. D., A. G. O. Form No. 55                                                    3—3104

This is the front side copy of an honorable discharge document from the Army of the United States of John D. Duresa by "Expiration Term of Service." It states that Duresa was born in Chicago, Illinois, and that he enlisted at "19-4" years of age. His occupation was listed as "Machinist Helper." He is documented as having blue eyes and blonde hair, with a height of "5 feet 6 3/4 inches." It was signed at Fort Sheridan by "C.C. Stuitt, Major 14th Cavalry" on June 14, 1933.

# ENLISTMENT RECORD

## OF

Duresa, John D., 6805094, Private
_(Last name)_ _(First name)_ _(Middle initial)_ _(Army Serial No.)_ _(Grade)_

Enlisted or ~~inducted~~, June 9th, 1930, at Chicago, Illinois

Completed __3__ years, __0__ months, __0__ days service for longevity pay.

Prior service: * __None__

Noncommissioned officer: __Never__

Qualification in arms: † __Marksman Rifle 9/22/32.__

Horsemanship: __Very Good__

Knowledge of any vocation: __Machinist Helper__

Attendance at: __None__
_(Name of noncommissioned officers' or special service school)_

Battles, engagements, skirmishes, expeditions: __None__

Decorations, service medals, citations: __None__

Wounds received in service: __None__

Physical condition when discharged: __Good__

Date and result of smallpox vaccination: ‡ __7/30/30 Vaccinia__

Date of completion of all typhoid-paratyphoid vaccinations: ‡ __8/13/30__

Date and result of diphtheria immunity test (Schick): ‡ __Not taken__

Date of other vaccinations (specify vaccine used): ‡ __Not taken__

Married or single: __Single__

Remarks: __Retained in service under 107th A WC (6 days) A.W.O.L. fr__
__O-L-30 to N-5-30 incl (2days) fr 7-10-32 to 7-10-32 incl (1 day), fr 8-1-32 to 8-2-32 incl (1 day),__
__fr 12-11-32 to 12-11-33 incl (1 day) fr 5-21-33 to 5-21-33 incl (1 day). Entitled to travel pay.__

Signature of soldier: __John D Duresa__

Character: __Excellent__

_Personnel Adjutant._

_(typed stamp, right side)_
Ft. Sheridan, Ill., June 14, 1933.
Sixteen & 45/100 Dollars.
Paid in full $ 16.45

John F. Connell
1st Lieut. Finance Dept.

Al Davis
Captain 14th Cavalry
Commanding Troops "B"

_* Give company, regiment, or branch, with inclusive dates of service in each enlistment._

---

Pictured here is the back side copy of the enlistment record of "Duresa, John D., 6805094, Private." He was enlisted on June 9, 1930, in Chicago, Illinois; his qualification in arms was documented as "Marksmanship Rifle 9/33/32." His horsemanship was "Very Good," and his vocation was listed as "Machinist Helper." There were no decorations, battles, or wounds to list. His marital status was "Single," and the date and result of his smallpox vaccination were filled out with "7/30/30 Vaccinia." The remarks say he was retained in service for a total of 12 days and entitled to travel pay. The typed portion was included at Fort Sheridan on June 14, 1933, and says, "Sixteen & 45/100 Dollars, paid in full $16.45"; it was approved by John F. Connell. Duresa was entitled to special pay, and his travel (extra) pay amounted to $1.37 a day.

61

This is a group photograph of the 14th Cavalry troops with friends and family members during a Christmas party in 1930 at Fort Sheridan. The soldier's families were invited to participate in a wonderful specially prepared meal and to socialize with the military staff. Special achievement awards for the new recruits were given out during this function.

These soldiers are taking advantage of their limited amount of leisure time. Pictured in the fort's recreation room with cavalrymen from the 14th Cavalry troop is Buster, their mascot, sitting on the pool table. Leisure time was also spent at saloons, restaurants, and entertainment centers in Highwood, located just outside the fort's entrance gates.

14TH U.S. CAVALRY REVIEW
FT SHERIDAN. ILL. 35 EKMARK

Sgt. Carl Ekmark, a very talented Army photographer from Texas, took this photograph of the 14th US Cavalry review at Fort Sheridan. He was able to capture an amazing view of the enormous parade grounds. A review of the troops, or a "pass," is a long-standing military tradition that began as a way for a newly assigned commander to inspect his troops. Visiting officers and guest speakers also were invited to review the troops. The fort's parade grounds are located north of the water tower complex and south of the target range and officers' club. It is evident that the 14th Cavalry practiced this formation often. The formation of mounted soldiers, whose movement is restricted by close-order maneuvering, is also known as "drilling." Most of these cavalry mounts are American Quarter Horses, one of the oldest recognized breeds of horses in the United States. These horses are favored because of their temperament, reliability, quickness, maneuverability, and stamina. Make note of the playful mascot dog between the officers and cavalrymen.

Pvt. John Duresa is one of the chefs on duty in these photographs at the fort's outdoor summer tent kitchen. The soldiers would have other duties in addition to battle drills, field exercises, and practicing for battle in the morning and afternoon. There would be planning and debriefing meetings, equipment maintenance, inspections, and advance-related coursework. There were fieldwork assignments to pick up litter and clear the brush on and around the post. Inside duties were usually in the barracks, consisting of sweeping, washing, waxing, and buffing the floors. In general, the soldiers had very little time to enjoy leisure activities.

Pictured is Duresa on outdoor kitchen duty peeling potatoes. The drill sergeant rotated the jobs every two weeks to all the enlisted soldiers. Most were assigned to the kitchen, laundry duties, or latrine responsibilities. Some others would have night guard duty. When the soldiers had spare time, they would play games like poker and dominoes. The men occasionally might find time to read or to write home.

This is a casual 1930s photograph taken of Pvt. John Duresa (left) with an unidentified fellow cavalryman. They appear to be standing in front of one of the officers' quarters or homes on Ronan Road, located on the north side of Fort Sheridan.

Private Duresa is pictured in his Army dress uniform as he stands in front of the Saddlers and Stable Sargent's building. Designed by Holabird and Roche in approximately 1891, it is located on Ronan Road at Fort Sheridan. The building is still there but now has been converted to a private residence.

A number of troops are shown here during their leisure time in the 1930s playing a game of catch. Tents were used at the fort during the spring and summer months for additional sleeping quarters. Extra accommodations would be needed during officer training camps and for new recruits of the induction center.

A souvenir photograph postcard titled "Off to Hollywood" was taken in 1933 of John Duresa (back center) with three unidentified cavalrymen and two women. They are at the Museum of Science and Industry's exhibit called Streets of Yesterday. The museum was constructed for Chicago's 1893 World Exposition and endowed by Julius Rosenwald, president of Sears Roebuck. He was a supporter of the Commercial Club of Chicago. The museum was open during Chicago's 1933 Century of Progress Exposition.

An unidentified officer poses at Fort Sheridan's drill field. A cavalry officer's horse was considered personal equipment and was transported with him to each assigned post. A little-known fact about cavalry horses is that they were known for their quickness, and often dispatchers and couriers chose the very best during wartime.

Private Duresa (right) is on a supply wagon pulled by four mules. A standard wagon body was 10 feet long, with a canvas top including the corps unit name and identification of the contents printed on it. The weight of a typical wooden wagon was about 1,300 pounds empty, and they would weigh more depending on the equipment packed inside.

A popular postcard purchased for 1¢ by the cavalrymen in the 1930s was available in the post's commissary store. The author is unknown. The postcard reads, "A girl shows her raisin when she makes a date with prune for whom she doesn't care a fig. She may be the apple of his eye, but she hands him a lemon, although she may have a cherry disposition. It is plum wrong, if her name be Anna he ought to ban Anna! By this time he would realize that his efforts has been fruitless."

*Four*

# ROUGH AND READY CAVALRYMEN

The US Army 14th Cavalry Regiment insignia motto, "Suivez Moi," is French, meaning "follow me," and has been used since its inception in 1901. The scroll with the inscription is below a yellow shield with a blue bend; a yellow cover and blue are used to reflect the color of the troopers' uniforms. The Kris blade and the rattlesnake represent service in the Philippines and Mexico. During the 1930s peacetime, the cavalry was involved in military training, equestrian competitions, and ceremonial exhibitions.

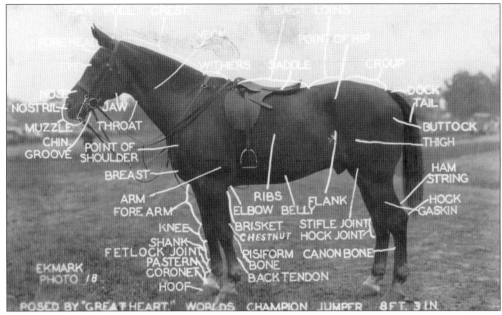

Pictured here is Great Heart, the world's greatest champion jumper, posing for the cavalry's basic training guide. Each arrow in the photograph indicates important anatomical landmarks of the horse. The cavalry training consisted of becoming extremely familiar with the horse assigned to the soldier. A soldier must be knowledgeable about the diseases of a horse, as it was an important part of their training. They were quizzed about the care for their horse before they could begin to ride it.

"The tougher the better they like it in the Army" is a fitting title for this photograph. Pvt. John Duresa (center), with other cavalrymen, is at a field demonstration of how to determine why a horse becomes suddenly lame. Trauma to the underside of a hoof is a common cause of lameness. A stone can cause a bruise and is a probable injury; it needs to be removed as soon as possible. Another typical problem is a loose horseshoe. Horses were the cavalrymen's most important commodity.

The "fire hurdle" jump in the 1930s, also referred to as "grid work," was the highlight of all the war games and tournaments at the fort and Soldier Field. This grid work is understood as essential to the training of the riders and their horses. Out on the battlefield, one never knows when a cavalryman would encounter a combination of a barbed-wire fence and a field fire for a horse to maneuver through. This type of training could prove to be worthwhile for the mounted troops. Not every horse could be eligible or qualify for the fire jump routine. A horse was required to be strong, swift, agile, obedient, and fearless. The following five consecutive photographs depict an exhibition of a fire hurdle jump.

All animals naturally are frightened of fire, but a well-trained horse is a great asset to the cavalry soldier. Jumping through an arch of fire was a display of the agility and discipline of both soldier and horse. The horse is expected to remain calm while the flames and embers appear to encompass them and while they carry out their routines. Demonstrations such as this one were provided free of charge to the public at Fort Sheridan and Soldier Field in Chicago. It raised the citizens' enthusiasm for the US military and exhibited the cavalry's readiness to defend the nation.

Here is the final photograph of the fire hurdle jump. On the left, the photographer is getting a good action shot of the cavalrymen and their horses. The public was grateful to the military for providing free entertainment since the Great Depression era brought an economic disaster. During this worldwide depression from 1929 to 1939, about 25 percent of the public was unemployed.

Another popular event at the fort was the competitive horse shows during the 1920s and 1930s. The "Roman over hurdle" was a show of bravery and horsemanship. The judge is stationed at the end of the hurdle watching each rider for any flaws in his performance. This rider appears to be rather confident in his routine.

Two cavalrymen are shown here using a horse as a shield. This maneuver, called "breastwork," is used as a temporary fortification when under enemy fire as a last resort in protecting oneself. Lt. Col. George Armstrong Custer used this course of action at his last and fatal battle at Little Bighorn in Montana Territory on June 25 and 26, 1876.

Another routine performed by the 14th Cavalry regularly was the "human hurdle." This photograph was taken at Fort Sheridan during the 1930s. All the events at the fort were held to build up the local citizens' enthusiasm for their military's keenness and quickness.

This is the 14th Cavalry review at Fort Sheridan photographed by Sgt. Carl Ekmark of Texas. The 1930s review is led by several of the officers at the fort's parade grounds. Practices with sabers were done on a regular basis to maintain the cavalrymen's discipline in control and direction while mounted on their horses. The soldiers were ordered to "display arms" with their sabers. They are leading the review with the marching band behind them, organizing their formation. The cavalry survived during the years of the Great Depression despite threats of increasing mechanization. The natural proponent for mechanization was the cavalry branch of the Army. Lack of funds sometimes halted new equipment purchases to replace the force's aging equipment. There was a limited amount of money to fix them during these lean times. When senior officers went up to Capitol Hill for funding, they knew that there might be a limit on money available to try new things. The officers tended to ask for what they could get. The cavalry survived more than 10 years after these troubling years.

The 14th Cavalry is on the parade grounds at the fort leading the garrison carrying the colors. According to regulations, each regiment carries two flags: the US silk flag and a wool bunting standard guidon flag with a cavalry number and company identification. The guidon flag measures about three by four feet with a swallowtail end and is carried on a lance about 10 feet long. There are four officers in the lead command of the troopers.

Here is the 14th Cavalry's second group of troops on the parade grounds with their sabers drawn. The rest of the garrison and the marching band are seen in the background. An interesting memorandum enacted by the military on February 15, 1934, discontinued the use of the cavalry saber. They were stored until further notice, with the US Cavalry ultimately dropping them as an item of regular war armament.

This is a closer view of B Company, 14th Cavalry, with Captain Gatchell in command riding on his white horse Jack. Gatchell had ordered arms, and the cavalrymen are holding their sabers appropriately. The troopers are shown here with their sabers drawn, resting on their right shoulder and balanced on their right thigh. The saber's primary function is as a slashing weapon. In history, a saber was especially popular among European and American cavalry soldiers. During the American Civil War, military-issued sabers were based on a French design featuring a slightly curved single-edged heavy carbon blade often referred to as the "old wrist-breaker." The sabers used in this photograph are a 1908 version, one that is lighter in weight and has a straight blade compared to the Civil War weapon. The popularity of cannons and muskets made sabers impractical in open battles during early wars. Today, cavalry sabers are symbolic and still worn as a sign of authority and tradition by some Army officers. In the background, the 5th Army Band is seen following the cavalry.

This is an assembly of one of the many parade exhibitions at Fort Sheridan. Pictured here with the 6th Army troopers is the 5th Army Band leading the parade for the day. The soldier bandsmen came from every part of the United States. The band was composed of professional musicians and career soldiers. As a result, the 5th Army Band offered its professional skill in promoting troop morale, supporting all military functions at Fort Sheridan, and promoting public relations within the city of Chicago. As time evolved, so did the Army musicians; they were offered many opportunities when leaving active duty for civilian life. Following the band is the infantry and then the cavalry. Here, the cavalry troops are in the middle of the formation in front of the heavy artillery, followed at the end by caissons and the artillery wagons driven by teams of mules.

The 14th Cavalry officers have ordered soldiers to "raise sabers." A saber is designed to be used only while mounted. The blade is used in heavy, hacking-like slashing blows. In this photograph, the officers are four lengths in front of their troops. The drill orders could be given either by voice or by trumpet.

Several mounted cavalry companies are pictured here, including Company B of the 14th. All are on the parade grounds of the fort in a rounding formation, most without their armament displayed. The cavalry played an important part in the defense of the nation. They were warriors who fought on horses and had the advantage of height, speed, and mobility in combat. The cavalry's role was reconnaissance, screening, and harassing the enemy.

The 14th Cavalry troop formation on the parade grounds at the fort has picked up their horses' pace to a moderate trot with sabers still drawn. These soldiers were very active and had a strong sense of engagement during this 1930s group photograph. They have an extreme amount of control over their horses. Each soldier is solely responsible for the care and well-being of his horse.

A drill at a war show performed by the 14th Cavalry was usually at the beginning of a parade or a review or after the marching band. These cavalrymen practiced weeks in advance of any event. Here, the soldiers have started a moderately fast pace with their horses and still maintain their close formation.

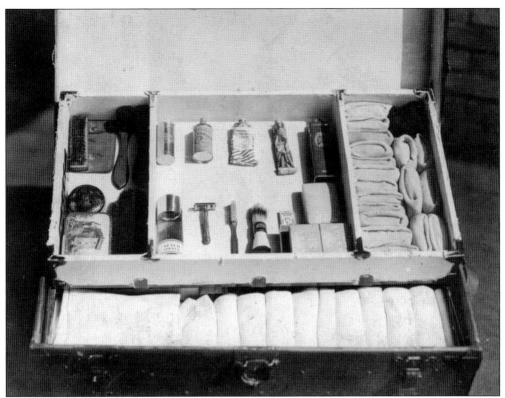

Fort Sheridan's 1930s government-issued US Army footlocker and clothes locker are shown here open and ready for inspection. This would be part of a regular barracks inspection conducted by the commanding officer of any US Army post and could be held at any time of day. Items were all folded and exhibited in a regulation-style manner. The cavalry troop's field equipment could be inspected just before its hike. A cavalry officer could inspect the horses' tack equipment at any time of the day.

A supply wagon pulled by four mules is pictured here at the end of a parade formation. It is driven by an unidentified soldier, and to his left is Pvt. John Duresa. The mule is a domestic equine hybrid breeding between a male donkey and a female horse. Although a mule was not as steady under fire as his half-brother the horse, they generally can pull heavier equipment. Mules live longer than horses and can easily maneuver rougher roads, survive on lower-grade feed, and are bred for their hardiness. Mules were used as pack animals, but could not run as fast as horses. Horses were better suited for artillery teams and ambulances during the Army cavalry days.

*Five*

# CHICAGO PARADES
# AND SOLDIER FIELD

Fort Sheridan troops held war shows and military tournaments at Soldier Field and parades in Chicago. The troops are traveling south on Columbus Drive to Soldier Field, led by Chicago police on motorcycles. The truck is carrying signs notifying the public about events. In the background is Chicago's skyline on North Michigan Avenue. The tallest and newest building is the Pittsfield; others are the Pure Oil, Wrigley, Carbide, Carbon, and London Guarantee Buildings.

The 14th Cavalry on parade is approaching the Art Institute on Michigan Avenue. Founded in 1879, it is one of the oldest and largest art museums in the United States. In the photograph's lower-right corner, the troops are nearing the first of two bronze sculptures known as the guard lions, each at a different pose. This lion at the south of the building "stands in an attitude of defiance" and was completed in 1894 by Chicago artist Edward Kemeys.

The cavalry troops are near the second bronze entrance guard lion on the north side of the building of the Art Institute. This lion "on the prowl" was also designed in 1894 by Chicagoan Edward Kemeys. In the background, the iconic Wrigley Building stands north at the end of the Michigan Avenue bridge. Numerous rippling American flags on the buildings show their patriotism and appreciation of the military.

Fort Sheridan's infantry troops are marching north on Michigan Avenue. As they near the corner of Washington Street, there are several large neon building signs that say "Frigidaire Product of General Motors." The company, founded in Fort Wayne, Indiana, developed the first refrigerators that were self-contained. In 1918, William C. Durant, founder of General Motors, invested in the company and named it Frigidaire. The three buildings shown are structurally the same as in the 1930s but without canvas awnings. This corner building is now a Walgreens.

The 14th Cavalry is on parade at 175 North State Street, heading north. The photograph was taken from the Lake Street Elevated train platform. On the left is the Chicago Theatre, built in 1921 for $4 million; it was the first lavish movie palace. Cornelius and George Rapp designed the theater. The front marquee is advertising "Talking Movies." American flags are seen on display from light poles and buildings commemorating the Fourth of July. In 1979, the Chicago Theatre was placed in the National Register of Historic Places.

The Fort Sheridan 14th Cavalry Regiment, Company B, is crossing over a Chicago bridge in June 1930 and headed south on its way to Soldier Field. The trip was over 26 miles and took around six and one-half hours of traveling on horseback. A horse normally travels about four miles per hour. This bridge has a wooden plank road surface.

The cavalry is turning off South Michigan Avenue and going toward Soldier Field. In the background is the Stevens Hotel, which went bankrupt due to the absence of substantial development during the Great Depression. During this era, Chicago was known as the center of recruiting in the Midwest. As a result, the Army purchased the Stevens Hotel for barracks, and the USO used the classrooms and ballrooms. Grant Park was used for drills and training. The Army sold the hotel in 1945 for $4.9 million to Conrad Hilton.

This is an early-1930s aerial view of South Michigan Avenue and Grant Park. The park, named in honor of US president Ulysses S. Grant, features a band shell and the Buckingham Fountain. The band shell shown in the lower portion of the photograph was constructed on a temporary basis at Ninth Street and Columbus Drive. Although temporary, it was the first formal structure located in Grant Park since the Lakefront Park Ballpark at Michigan Avenue and Madison Street from 1879 to 1884. The positive impact of the park on South Michigan Avenue's real estate resulted in higher gains in value compared to the north side of Michigan Avenue. The park is a component of the 57-acre Museum Campus, consisting of the Adler Planetarium, the Field Museum of Natural History, Soldier Field, and the Shedd Aquarium, all built on a landfill. Grant Park is a large urban park in Chicago's downtown Loop area. Within South Michigan Avenue is the city's central business district across from Grant Park.

The 14th Cavalry is currently traveling south down Lake Shore Drive in front of the Field Museum, located on the Museum Campus, and on the move to Soldier Field. The Army exhibitions were held at Soldier Field several times a year. They were offered free of charge to the public due to the ongoing Great Depression.

The cavalrymen have arrived at their final destination, Soldier Field. The entire expansive east side of Soldier Field is seen in this photograph. It was a total 33-mile trip on horseback from Fort Sheridan and could take about eight and one-quarter hours, not including rest stops.

The entire 14th Cavalry Regiment has arrived on the Museum Campus after traveling on South Lake Shore Drive heading toward Soldier Field. It appears like some automobile traffic has stopped to watch the troops' arrival.

The 14th Cavalry is passing the Field Museum and still making its way to Soldier Field. Most of the officers are walking their horses while the automobiles are rounding up the end line of the troops. It has been a long tiring ride for all, including their horses.

The battle act photograph was taken from an airship balloon used for the war tournament in June 1930. The arena was designed in 1919 by the architectural firm Holabird & Roche as a horseshoe-shaped stadium in Neoclassical style with matching Doric colonnades. The stadium opened on October 9, 1924, as the Grant Park Municipal Stadium. Later, on November 11, 1925, it was renamed Soldier Field in honor of American soldiers who died in combat. Both the Field Museum and Soldier Field are on Chicago's lakefront and part of the Museum Campus. Soldier Field was the largest war memorial in the world. The distinctive Neoclassical columns designed to complement the Field Museum building's architecture are seen at the north open end of the field. In early construction, the plans for the museum were altered to allow it to act as a hospital for World War I, but the government canceled it. It finally opened in 1921, and Soldier Field was formally dedicated on November 27, 1927.

Fort Sheridan troops are shown in 1930 at Soldier Field in their sleeping quarters under the main arena seating area. The soldiers hung their clothes from metal pipes with ropes wrapped around the pillars. Bathrooms and kitchen facilities were conveniently located nearby. The soldiers usually stayed a minimum of a week for each of the war exhibitions.

This is the opening ceremony of the military tournament and war show at Soldier Field that took place June 21–29, 1930. All Fort Sheridan Army regiments are in attendance, including the 14th Cavalry. Exhibitions during the Great Depression were promoted by the military and the United States of America and were intended to be uplifting to the public during rough economic times.

The war shows were part of the military department's program to stimulate interest in national defense and speed up enrollment in the citizens' military training camps. Here, Company B cavalry troops of Fort Sheridan are in the center arena for their demonstration. A large throng of spectators has formed, and all appear to be enjoying the precision drills of the cavalry.

Shown here in 1930 is the entire 14th Cavalry Regiment demonstrating lancer drill routines in Soldier Field's center exhibition arena. A lance can be somewhat of an awkward pole weapon usually 10 to 12 feet long and designed to be used by a mounted cavalryman.

Soldier Field is hosting the second US Infantry military war tournament on June 21–29, 1930. The opening ceremony had always started with a parade of all of America's past and present armies. In the lead are the Revolutionary War soldiers, followed by the War of 1812, and then the Civil War uniformed soldiers. The World War I soldier group is next. All the uniformed armies are passing by the reviewing stand, where several generals of the Army are in attendance. The spectators are standing and honoring the American flag and applauding the soldiers coming into view. The stands appear full, and the audience is jubilant.

Leading here is 14th Cavalry, A Troop, of Fort Sheridan taking its position in the military tournament parade at Soldier Field June 21–29, 1930. The troop features about 30 trick cavalrymen standing on their horses. This parade is well attended by a sea of onlookers. The audience honors the American flag as it passes by. Parades such as this exhibit the military strength of the country of that era. In the background are the famous Soldier Field's Neoclassical-style architecture facades. Soldier Field is a longtime Chicago historic landmark.

Next at the opening ceremony is the 14th Cavalry, B Troop, of Fort Sheridan carrying the American flag at the lineup. The military marching band follows the cavalry playing ceremonial marching music, including national anthems and patriotic songs. Each company is carrying the American flag and their troop's flag. Everyone is passing by the general and his guests in the reviewing stand during the war tournament in June 1930. The stands are overflowing with a crowd of onlookers.

Soldiers of Fort Sheridan's 6th Corps Army battalion practice their well-disciplined formations before the 8:00 p.m. show. The infantry is in perfect form in front of the military marching band. The 6th Corps sponsored the first of many military pageants in May 1925 at Soldier Field. These war shows established the blueprint for future demonstrations that followed over the next 20 years.

At the Soldier Field arena, troops from the A and B Companies of the 14th Cavalry of Fort Sheridan are pictured here practicing before the evening performance of the war show in 1930. The heavy artillery and caissons as a rule follow the cavalry in the night performances.

In the center arena is the cavalry's B Troop demonstrating its skillful exercises at Soldier Field with lances. The cavalrymen, while mounted on a horse, used lances. They are usually 10 feet long and can be somewhat burdensome, but cavalrymen are still trained to use them. Behind the cavalry is the heavy artillery firing blank shells. Spectators were thrilled to witness this event with the thunderous boom of cannons.

This is a close-action photograph of the cavalry's B Troop performing in the afternoon with its lance charge drills in the center arena. The tips of the lances usually have a sharp metal tip, but these have a blunt tip. The lances were phased out at this time and only used for exhibitions.

A 1930 photograph shows cavalry exhibiting their lances in a charge position viewed by a few onlookers in the stands. Prior to the outbreak of World War I, there had been controversy as to whether lances or sabers were the more effective for cavalry, but neither proved a match for modern 1930s firearms.

Shown here is a drill of lance use followed by a charge command during a war show in 1930. The thundering hoofs of the horses and lances are most effectively used from behind the enemy, with a striking position on their left side. This style of equipment proved to be clumsy and easily deflected when compared to sabers. Fort Sheridan's infantry is seen in the lower-right foreground, with bayonets on the rifles, in an attack drill.

Pictured is another spectacular and action-packed display by the 14th Cavalry, B Troop, of the fire jump at the opening ceremony. The flames and smoke generated by the fire were often a health issue and sometimes dangerous to the soldier and his horse. Various jumps were practiced and performed on a regular basis at Fort Sheridan.

The 6th Corps cavalry soldiers and their horses jump through the arch of flames. Jumping through fire was an exhibit of the agility and discipline of both soldiers as well their well-trained horses. All animals are naturally frightened of fire, but a well-trained steed is of great value to the cavalryman.

This is the conclusion of the "Battle Act Military Tournament" at Soldier Field in Chicago. Actual live field artillery was not used during the evening demonstrations. This was a ground-shaking, heart-throbbing event for all who attended. The nighttime atmosphere emphasized the firepower of the cannons and the smoke from the machine artillery.

This is the 6th Army Corps demonstration portion of the war show of 1930. The men usually performed near dusk, just before the heavy artillery demonstrations. Infantry battalions from Fort Sheridan, Jefferson Barracks, and Missouri demonstrate their readiness together with a combined group of trained troops from other Army posts.

Shown here is the troops' evening war show of 1930. With so much artillery firing, it is creating a thick smoke screen and still maintaining the "boom" despite the lack of bullets inside shells. This exhibit is the most ear-deafening sound of the entire show, but the evening cannon demonstrations draw the biggest crowds. The only thing better than this would be actual battlefield action.

This is an evening war show with all the field artillery in the center arena of Soldier Field. Cannons were continually firing, making a thick smoke screen. These evening demonstrations were action-packed and thrilling to the spectators. Only ammunition cartridges without bullets inside were used. This was a demonstration of the nation's war equipment and the readiness of the soldiers to protect the country if needed.

The battle act and military evening tournament at Soldier Field was held June 21–29, 1930. Soldier Field hosted this weeklong tournament that included aerial demonstrations, battle scenes and artillery demonstrations, a parade, and pyrotechnic displays. This venue was tailor-made for such a tournament, as Soldier Field was constructed to honor soldiers and military veterans.

This is a 1930s war show battle scene showing a display of cannon power at night. The soldiers held mock battles using blank-filled cartridges in the cannons and tanks at the evening shows. It was an excellent training tool for the soldiers to battle-test their newer equipment. The war battles and tournaments were probably some of the more spectacular shows prior to World War II.

This is the end of the battle act during the military tournament that took place June 21–29, 1930. In the background is a mock city backdrop staging for war re-enactments and performances. In the background is the Field Museum, built in 1921. Early plans were revised to use this building as a World War I hospital, but that never happened. As it stands, the building is one of the largest museums of natural history in the United States.

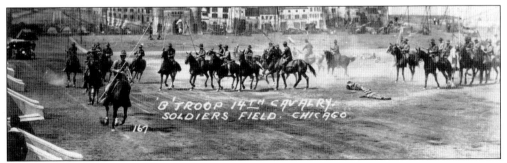

Pictured here is 14th Cavalry, B Troop, at Soldier Field in 1930. The troop is practicing its precision drill formations. In the background, canvas sheets are seen with painted special effects on them. The canvas inserts are being set up for use in the military tournament competition in the center arena.

This photograph, titled "Buster Going in the Balloon in Big Company," was taken at Soldier Field in Chicago during one of the war game demonstrations. In the balloon basket with Buster the dog is Roscoe "Fatty" Arbuckle, who was a famous silent film actor, comedian, director, and screenwriter of the 1920s. Fatty started his career at Selig Polyscope Company and later moved to Keystone Studios in Hollywood. He mentored Charlie Chaplin (1889–1977) and discovered Buster Keaton (1895–1966), Monty Banks (1897–1950), and Bob Hope (1903–2003). Arbuckle was one of Hollywood's highest-paid actors of the time. The man at Fatty's right is Will Hays, a Hollywood producer and friend. The other occupants in the balloon are unidentified.

The grand parade at Soldier Field was photographed on June 24, 1932, during George Washington's bicentennial birthday celebration. All the troops of Fort Sheridan are in the arena, including the infantry and the cavalry. All have passed by the general and his guests at the reviewing stand. The Navy's sailors from Great Lakes Naval Base can be seen. In the 1930s, the Navy was the largest branch of the US military. At the rear of the parade is the field artillery, machine guns, and cannons. Organizers of these demonstrations brought in all the best available fighting equipment, including 1,000 soldiers, 500 horses, 8 tanks, and 12 airplanes, along with several airship dirigibles. The show included marching, but that wasn't what the public flocked to see, it was the mock battles. The war games were the biggest attraction and were admission-free during the Great Depression. Events such as these were part of the military department's program to stimulate interest in national defense and speed up enrollment in the citizens' military training camps. Fort Sheridan was one of the Midwest's largest training and enlistment center camps of the time.

The Army's "flying aces" are in a pursuit formation over Soldier Field. An aerial display was always a highlight of the war tournaments. In 1932, the show welcomed Amelia Earhart, an American aviation pioneer. Amelia was among those in the reviewing stands at the George Washington bicentennial military tournament held at Soldier Field on June 24, 1932.

Shown here is a single aircraft from the group of the Army's flying aces of the US Air Corps performing tumbling and rolling maneuvers. This biplane is creating a smoke screen to conceal or mask its location from any ground enemy during wartime. Other air features were group air jumping, trick aircraft maneuvers, and combined formations of pursuit. These were a hallmark in most of the war tournaments at the Soldier Field.

The air show entertainment always treated the audience to an electrifying aerial demonstration. This squadron of biplanes is from the Army's flying aces. This show brought thrilling maneuvers of aircraft acrobatics, including the spectacular looping of the Comet by a propeller-driven biplane, parachute jumping, and combined arrow attack mode formations. This was featured in all of the war tournaments at Soldier Field. Aircraft use was starting to evolve during the 1920s and 1930s, after World War I and before World War II.

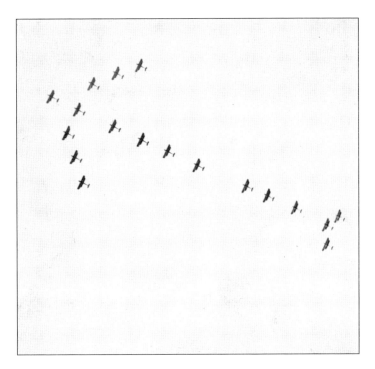

Featured is the E Battalion of Fort Sheridan during a 1930 military tournament at Soldier Field. In the arena, an exhibition of the battle act is seen from the spectator stands. The war battles and tournaments were some of the more spectacular shows of arms power prior to World War II. Their performance was a much-loved event by the public.

REGULAR ARMY TROOPS, 6TH CORPS AREA.
GEORGE WASHINGTON BI-CENTENNIAL MILITARY TOURNAMENT,
SOLDIERS FIELD, CHICAGO, JUNE 24TH TO JULY 4TH 1932.
EKMARK PHOTO. 231

Featured here is the grand opening parade of George Washington's bicentennial birthday celebration. It was held from June 24 to July 4, 1932, at Soldier Field. Pictured are the Regular Army 6th Corps troops, including their full arms and equipment. The troops on parade was a presentation of all participating military units and equipment to present for inspection by the general in charge of the event. The best of the Army's implements of war are inspected and ceremonially approved before the start of an evening's events. Followed by the grand parade was an air show with a flyover by four squadrons of fighter planes escorted by a plane flown by Amelia Earhart. Her aircraft was painted to resemble a red and white eagle. Earhart later landed and made her way to the stadium, where she was given a gold medal and spoke to the crowd (as well as an audience listening to a radio broadcast of the event) about her flight across the Atlantic the previous year. She graduated from Chicago's Hyde Park Academy High School in 1915.

All the 14th Cavalry soldiers are waiting to appear in the evening ceremony of the George Washington bicentennial birthday celebration in 1932. The official commemoration logo of Washington's profile shadow is on the grandstand banners.

This photograph was taken during the George Washington bicentennial birthday celebration sometime from June 24 to July 4, 1932. Pictured is an assembly of the grand entry of all the troops of Fort Sheridan, including motorized Army warfare. The soldiers are standing for a formal assessment or evaluation by the generals at the reviewing stand. In the background, the Field Museum is seen with similar architectural details of Soldier Field, designed to complement the museum.

Pictured is a helium-filled barrage balloon with a basket taking off from Soldier Field. The men on the ground are guiding its ascension. The US military was not always interested in barrage balloons, and the program took some years to develop. The development of barrage balloons began during World War I and was undertaken by many European nations during the war. In the background are holding racks for the cannon shells. Behind the artillery is a grouping of soldiers' tents.

Crowds of visitors are touring the military tent camp at Soldier Field in 1932. The public had an opportunity to review the equipment the Army uses. In the background, the Chicago World's Fair of 1933 is about to open. Fort Sheridan troops came back to Soldier Field for the grand opening celebration of the Chicago World's Fair.

# Six

# HIKES AND FIELD TRIPS

Cavalry hikes were throughout Illinois and Wisconsin, and the cavalry often held war shows and demonstrations at each encampment. In the 1930s, the cavalry journeyed from Fort Sheridan 22 miles to Grayslake. The troops are traveling north on Half Day Road in this photograph. The village was named after William Gray, an early landowner from New York. He purchased land by the then-unnamed lake. It is assumed that is how the lake and village got their names. The names "Grays" and "Lake" were joined together for the post office's convenience.

Company B of the 14th Cavalry is headed north on Route 83 to Grayslake, riding parallel to railroad tracks owned in the 1930s by the Wisconsin Central Railway Company. Little development occurred in Grayslake until the railroad line was built. The railroad erected a station in July 1886, naming it Grays Lake and later combining the two words to "Grayslake." Typical of the development of other communities in the area, reasonable land prices and easy rail transportation brought the big city of Chicago closer to the rural areas. These advantages all served as a magnet to soldiers returning from war who sought a less-urban atmosphere to raise families. Horsepower in rural areas was more reliable than automobiles since there were fewer filling stations around. Soldiers here are traveling on the edges of the road for safety reasons, leaving the center for automobiles to pass. The cavalry's mule-powered wagons are carrying supplies for the horses, food staples, camp shelters, and artillery. Grayslake was a day trip for the soldiers.

The cavalrymen and wagons pictured are on the journey to Grayslake, riding parallel to the railroad tracks to the right. In alignment with the railroad tracks are track-side signals and telegraph poles. The telegraph poles of the 1930s carried information about the train's arrival time on wires constructed of copper. The poles could also carry telephone and electrical wires. As time passed, fewer poles and wires were needed, so the poles were eventually discontinued. Some old, abandoned poles are seen beside the railway tracks today.

The troops pass by local restaurants in the background. Mike's Barbecue advertises a "1/2 chicken and French fries" meal special. Behind the building is a garage repair shop, and beyond is a sign advertising Shorewood Gulf Club and Bart's Restaurant and Barbecue. Bart's is where Charlotte Renehan, a Grayslake historian, worked while in high school. All restaurants pictured have been demolished. The land is now vacant and for sale.

The troops are riding toward Grayslake, having passed by several restaurants in the background. All the buildings are on the east side of Route 83 and opposite the railroad track. This is another view of Mike's Barbecue. An adjoining automobile repair garage and a gas station features a logo sign. In the far distance, Bart's Restaurant and Barbecue are in view.

All the troops have arrived at the Grayslake camp area. This trip takes nearly a day on horseback. First on their agenda was caring for their horses. Each soldier carried a tent and personal items on his horse. The extra weight usually added about 50 to 60 pounds more for the horse to carry.

Tents are up, and the horses are covered for the night's stay in Grayslake in 1932. On the far right of the photograph is the "Mule Barn," which was demolished. Charlotte Renehan, Grayslake's historian, said the site now has a bank. In the background is Grayslake's water storage tank, and in the center left of the photograph, between trees, is the 1920s brick stack of Grayslake's gelatin factory. Both are still part of the current skyline.

A hearty meal appears to be ready, and the soldiers are enjoying their time to rest after a day of events. Photographers often travel with the soldiers. Commanders often choose talented soldiers from the Army ranks and make them regimental photographers. A great number of photographs of Fort Sheridan troops were taken by Sgt. Carl J. Ekmark, a regimental photographer of the 14th Cavalry.

The soldier's teepee-style tents are pitched in an area near the location of their performance field. Some tents were used to shelter cannon caissons and their artillery. Others are used to cover supplies for the cooks and the soldiers' war show equipment. All the horses here have been fed and watered and will be tied to hitching posts for the night. Army wagons have been unloaded at "Grays Lake Camp" in 1932.

It is "Chow Time in the Field" for the 14th Cavalry. All the trucks, chuck wagons, dining equipment, and tents are pictured at Grayslake's temporary cavalry camp. The soldiers have eaten and are planning for their next day of events. Tomorrow, the troops will probably be in another town to promote the Army.

In September 1930, the troops visited Lake Lauderdale, Wisconsin, which was about a 75-mile, two-day hike from Fort Sheridan. The cavalry's purpose for these field trips was to demonstrate the newest fighting equipment and the ability of the troops to protect the nation. Here, the cavalry is getting the horses ready for the night. Caring for the horses comes first, and this was their most important asset. The troops watered their horses at the lake and set up camp behind the cottages. The lake was named after James Lauderdale, who moved to the area in 1841 with his family. The New York native built the first residential building in 1842. James's brother-in-law and cousin purchased 160 acres each under the Homestead Act for the price of $1.25 an acre. Prior to the 1900s, Lauderdale Lake was sparsely populated, compared to the 1930s. Businessmen who lived in nearby towns bought the lakefront property and built modest cottages and cabins for their summer use. Families built houses themselves, while others were able to jump-start the construction process between the wars and purchase decommissioned Army buildings from Camp Grant in Rockford, Illinois.

This is a group photograph of the cavalrymen getting ready for camp at Lake Lauderdale. Pvt. John Duresa is in front of Captain Gatchell's white horse Jack. The horses will be fed and watered before anything else gets done. The saddles are off, and the horses will be brushed, since all were on a dusty trail through the weeds and underbrush.

The 14th Cavalry, Troop B, got its horses ready for a stay at Lake Lauderdale. The next chore is to get the camp ready for the soldiers' stay after a fatiguing hike. The men have a chance to pose for a photograph, making sure their mascot dogs are in the picture. It has been a long two-day trip to get here in 1930.

The horses have been given water and feed and are unsaddled in the background. Now the cavalrymen can pitch their tents and get ready for their night's stay. They will be getting up at 5:00 a.m. at the bugler's call tomorrow for another day of events.

Only a team of two men is needed to peel potatoes for "K.P." (Kitchen Police) duty on the hike. There are still some preparations to do before dinnertime and finally bedtime. In the background is the exhibition field at Powers Lake. Most of their wagons have been stored there until the next day of exhibitions.

It is chow time, and the troops are in line at Lake Lauderdale. It has been a long day for the men and their horses. Now, there is time to eat, rest, and relax under the cool shade of the tall evergreen trees. The horses are all tied and ready for the night.

Pictured is chow time at Lake Lauderdale. The cavalrymen are settled on the ground, enjoying their meal. One soldier has time to make sure the mascot dog is posing for the photographer. The mascot dogs became very attached to the soldiers and longed to be with them, even on hikes. The Fort Sheridan Post Cemetery has a dog buried there who died of a broken heart because he could not travel with the troops.

In the background, the tents are set up, and it is time to wait for dinner. The men have time for a few smiles for the camera. There is even time to ride a horse through the camp. It is the end of another exhausting day of performances.

The 5:00 a.m. reveille bugle wake-up call has been sounded. This is "Some Dusty Place" for the 14th Cavalry getting up this particular morning. It appears to be a little cool at Lake Lauderdale in September 1930. Here, the troops are on the move to the next encampment and the next town's war demonstration.

The entire 14th Cavalry Regiment has arrived at Powers Lake from Fort Sheridan after a long 47-mile hike. The soldiers are watering the horses at the lake. Powers Lake is located in Kenosha, Walworth County, Wisconsin. The photographs depict the area as a resort-type atmosphere. In the background is a large water slide. This area was originally called Lakeville, then Nippersink, and later, Powers Lake. It is named after James B. Powers, one of its early settlers, and the town's first postmaster. The area was a farming community that appreciated the fertile Wisconsin soil and access to a good water supply. The natural resources were especially conducive to wheat growing in the 1870s; the Chicago Railway system sent three trains a day from Chicago to Powers Lake for the farmers to send their grains for processing back to the city. This connection to Chicago helped Wisconsin expand its agricultural opportunities.

At Powers Lake, a very important detail is digging holes for a latrine and the disposal of waste materials in the field. All these chores need to be done before dinner. It seems they will be in this town for a few days to promote the military.

A group of soldiers is waiting in line to unload the chow camp wagon and supplies at Powers Lake. First, the tents, followed by the chow wagon, need to be unloaded so the cooks can start dinner for the night. Occasionally, the troops would discuss and plan for the next day's war tournaments and demonstrations.

The horses have been fed and watered. In addition, the men would unload feed and hay from the wagons for their horses. The next chore for the soldiers is to find a good spot for the tents before they can eat dinner. A grouping of supply wagons is pictured in the background. Often, the residents of the towns the soldiers visited would bring local produce and homemade items for the soldiers to enjoy.

All the cavalrymen are pitching their tents for the night's stay at Powers Lake. The cavalrymen's horses have to be watered and fed and are ready for the night's stay. The supply and artillery wagons are seen in the background. The wagons are unloaded, inspected, and inventoried before the day is over.

It appears as if all the tents are up for the night. The pennants for the 14th Cavalry, B Troop, are seen hung on a lance stuck in the ground. The troops are anxiously awaiting the next activity, chow time, and then bedtime.

Chow time is called for the 14th Cavalry with a "come and get it." No one needs the invitation to have a meal at a table; the troops seem quite comfortable sitting on the ground, eating under the shade of the trees. It is time for a well-desired rest and meal.

Both companies of Troops A and B are in the field at Powers Lake. "Come and Get It" is the title of this photograph. Finally, after a long day of demonstrations, the soldiers are forming the chow line. After eating, plans for the next day's trip will be discussed.

All the cavalrymen have finally eaten, and it is time to relax in the field. This has been a long day in 1930 for the soldiers. There is a number of trucks in this photograph. Prior to this, there was probably a demonstration or parade at Powers Lake for the soldiers to participate in. In the foreground, two soldiers play records on a phonograph. It appears the troops have ended their stay at Powers Lake and are returning to Fort Sheridan soon.

In 1932, the 14th Cavalry hiked 22 miles west on Route 22 to its end at Northwest Highway to the village of Fox River Grove, Illinois, incorporated in 1919 and originally settled by Bohemian-born Frank Opatrny. Chicagoans traveled by train and auto to enjoy this peaceful resort area by the Fox River. The picnic grove welcomed its first luxury hotel in 1902, a wonderful beach area, and a dance pavilion in the 1920s on Northwest Highway. The village had McHenry County's first movie theater, built in 1925, featuring silent and talking films. The historic movie theater building has been gutted and will be demolished soon. Below is the troop's camp with two cavalrymen peeling potatoes and a woman visitor sitting on a chair. Several soldiers are onlookers posing for the picture. One of the cavalrymen is holding a young child. The mascots on this trip are Butch and Laddy.

# DISCOVER THOUSANDS OF LOCAL HISTORY BOOKS FEATURING MILLIONS OF VINTAGE IMAGES

Arcadia Publishing, the leading local history publisher in the United States, is committed to making history accessible and meaningful through publishing books that celebrate and preserve the heritage of America's people and places.

Find more books like this at
## www.arcadiapublishing.com

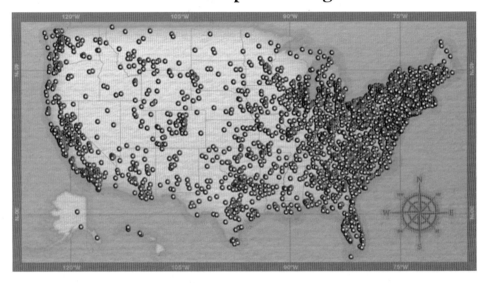

Search for your hometown history, your old stomping grounds, and even your favorite sports team.

Consistent with our mission to preserve history on a local level, this book was printed in South Carolina on American-made paper and manufactured entirely in the United States. Products carrying the accredited Forest Stewardship Council (FSC) label are printed on 100 percent FSC-certified paper.

MADE IN THE USA